PSALTER FOR WORSHIP

Cycle C

Revised Common Lectionary

Psalter for Worship
Cycle C

Revised Common Lectionary

Augsburg Fortress
Minneapolis

PSALTER FOR WORSHIP, CYCLE C
The Revised Common Lectionary

Editor: Martin A. Seltz
Production editor: Lani Willis

Material from the following sources is acknowledged:

Lutheran Book of Worship, © 1978 Lutheran Church in America, The American Lutheran Church, The Evangelical Lutheran Church of Canada, and The Lutheran Church-Missouri Synod.

With One Voice Leaders Edition, © 1995 Augsburg Fortress.

The Revised Common Lectionary, © 1992 Consultation on Common Texts.

Book of Common Prayer (1979).

Seasonal Psalms, © 1978 Augsburg Publishing House.

Manufactured in U.S.A.   ISBN 0-8066-3576-2   AF 3-555

1   2   3   4   5   6   7   8   9   0

Also available:
PSALTER FOR WORSHIP: CYCLE B (3-554)

LECTIONARY TABLES
Readings and Prayers (3-388)
A table of Revised Common Lectionary readings with LBW Prayers of the Day.
With One Voice Leaders Edition (3-302)
This supplementary Lutheran worship resource contains a table of Revised Common Lectionary readings paired with propers from LBW.
Between Sundays (3-401)
A three-year table of daily Bible readings related to the Revised Common Lectionary.

LECTIONARY VOLUMES
Lectionary for Worship, Cycle C (3-383)
Complete Revised Common Lectionary readings for Cycle C, sense-lined to facilitate public reading. NRSV translation.
Lectionary for Worship, Ritual Edition (3-384)
Hardcover volume containing complete Revised Common Lectionary readings for all three lectionary cycles (A, B, C), sense-lined to facilitate public reading. NRSV.
Readings for the Assembly, Cycle C (3-397)
Revised Common Lectionary readings for Cycle C, sense-lined to facilitate public reading. Based on the NRSV and incorporating inclusive language for God.

CALENDAR RESOURCES (REVISED COMMON LECTIONARY)
Church Year Calendar
Calendar-dated table of readings for Sundays and festivals.
Liturgical Wall Calendar
Full-color 13-month calendar with readings for Sundays and festivals.
Liturgical Planning Calendar for the Church Year
A worship planning guide, daily devotional, and appointment calendar based on the Revised Common Lectionary and *Lutheran Book of Worship.*

WORSHIP RESOURCES FOR CONGREGATIONAL AND HOME USE
Sundays and Seasons Worship Planning Guide, Year of Luke, Cycle C (3-1202)
Calendar-dated guide providing materials needed to prepare worship for Sundays and seasons. Based on the Revised Common Lectionary.
Welcome Home: Scripture, Prayers, and Blessings for the Household, Year of Luke (10-33298)
Practical resource for daily prayer in the home. Based on the Revised Common Lectionary.
Indexes for Worship Planning (3-400)
Reference tools for hymn selection and worship preparation based on *Lutheran Book of Worship, With One Voice,* and the Revised Common Lectionary.

Contents

Preface

Psalter for Worship is designed to support congregational singing of the psalms, especially among those who use the Revised Common Lectionary. This volume of *Psalter for Worship* includes psalms for Sundays and holy days in Cycle C. Included also are the complete set of resources for the Vigil of Easter, and psalms for lesser festivals and occasions as listed in *Lutheran Book of Worship* and *With One Voice.*

The psalms presented here are those appointed in the *Revised Common Lectionary* to accompany the set of first readings that correlate with the Gospel readings. Where the *RCL* offers several alternate psalms, one has been chosen for this resource. Each psalm is paired with a refrain, a succinct psalm excerpt that lifts up an image or theme central to the day for which it is chosen. (The complete set of refrain texts is published in *With One Voice Leaders Edition*, pp. 74–120; the psalm translation and versification is that of *Book of Common Prayer*, used also in *Lutheran Book of Worship*.)

Psalter for Worship supports the psalm settings in Augsburg Fortress lectionary inserts *(Celebrate* and *Jubilate)*. Accompaniments for refrains and psalm tones along with the complete psalm texts are printed together here to facilitate psalm singing. In addition, this volume provides newly composed alternate psalm tones for most of the psalms. *Psalter for Worship* may also be used independently of the lectionary inserts by using the reproducible refrains and/or tones for congregational participation printed beginning on page 121. Sufficient copies of this volume are needed for use by musical leaders.

These psalm settings may be used in a variety of ways, from simple to more elaborate. Here are just a few possibilities:

–Choir or cantor introduces the refrain; the congregation repeats it. Choir/cantor then alternates with the congregation on the verses (alternation is by whole verses). Subsequent refrains are sung once by all.

–Same treatment of the refrain; the choir, or the congregation, sings all the verses of the psalm.

–Organ or other keyboard accompaniment may be used on the refrain; the verses may be sung with or without accompaniment.

–Handbell parts and vocal/instrumental descants (all of which are optional in these settings) may be added. The melody line of the refrain may be doubled by an instrument to support the congregation's singing.

–When a double psalm tone is used (such as *LBW* 6–10), boldface type is ignored and the psalm is sung in groups of two verses. An extra single verse at the end of a psalm may be sung to the second half of the tone (usually by choir or cantor).

–Choir or congregation sings the refrain in harmony (where provided) with or without accompaniment.

Further information on psalm singing may be found in *Lutheran Book of Worship*, pp. 290–291. Accompaniments for all the *LBW* psalm tones are in *Lutheran Book of Worship: Accompaniment Edition—Liturgy*, pp. 123–125.

A complete index of the composers for this volume and their contributions begins on page 156.

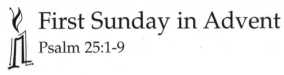

First Sunday in Advent
Psalm 25:1-9

Refrain

Carolyn Jennings

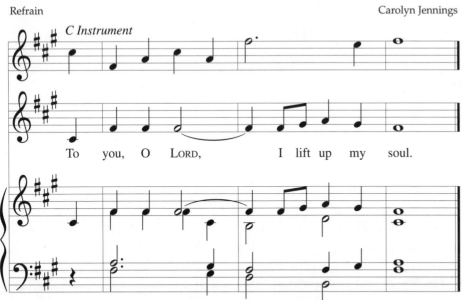

To you, O LORD, I lift up my soul.

[1]To you, O LORD, I lift up my soul; my God, I put my trust in you;*
let me not be humiliated, nor let my enemies triumph over me.
   [2]Let none who look to you be put to shame;*
   let the treacherous be disappointed in their schemes. ℞
[3]Show me your ways, O LORD,*
and teach me your paths.
   [4]Lead me in your truth and teach me,*
   for you are the God of my salvation;
   in you have I trusted all the day long.
[5]Remember, O LORD, your compassion and love,*
for they are from everlasting.
   [6]Remember not the sins of my youth and my transgressions;*
   remember me according to your love
   and for the sake of your goodness, O LORD. ℞
[7]Gracious and upright is the LORD;*
therefore he teaches sinners in his way.
   [8]He guides the humble in doing right*
   and teaches his way to the lowly.
[9]All the paths of the LORD are love and faithfulness*
to those who keep his covenant and his testimonies. ℞

Second Sunday in Advent
Luke 1:68-79

Refrain

Carolyn Jennings

Handbells

C Instrument

In the ten - der com - pas - sion of our God, the dawn from on high shall break up - on us.

Psalm tone

⁶⁸Blessed be the Lord, the Gód of Israel;*
he has come to his people and śet them free.
  ⁶⁹He has raised up for us a mighty Savior,*
  born of the house of his śervant David. ℞
⁷⁰Through his holy prophets he promised of old
⁷¹that he would save us from our enemies,*
from the hands of áll who hate us.
  ⁷²He promised to show mercy ío our fathers*
  and to remember his hóly covenant.
⁷³This was the oath he swore to our fáther Abraham:*
to set us free from the hands óf our enemies,
  free to worship him without fear,*
  ⁷⁵holy and righteous in his sight
  all the days óf our life. ℞
⁷⁶You, my child, shall be called the prophet of íhe Most High*
for you will go before the Lord to prepáre his way,
  ⁷⁷to give his people knowledge óf salvation*
  by the forgiveness óf their sins.
⁷⁸In the tender compassion óf our God*
the dawn from on high shall bréak upon us,
  ⁷⁹to shine on those who dwell in darkness and the shadow of death,*
  and to guide our feet into the way of peace. ℞

Alternate tone

PFW 42

Third Sunday in Advent
Isaiah 12:2-6

Refrain

Carolyn Jennings

In your midst is the Ho - ly One of Is - ra - el.

2 octaves
Handbells used: 9

2Surely God is my salvation;*
I will trust, and will not be afraid,
  for the LORD GOD is my strength and my might;*
  he has become my salvation. ℟
3With joy you will draw water*
from the wells of salvation.
  4And you will say in that day:*
  Give thanks to the LORD, call on his name;
make known his deeds among the nations;
proclaim that his name is exalted.
  5Sing praises to the LORD, for he has done gloriously;*
  let this be known in all the earth.
6Shout aloud and sing for joy, O royal Zion,
for great in your midst is the Holy One of Israel. ℟

Fourth Sunday in Advent

Luke 1:47-55

Refrain

Carolyn Jennings

The LORD has lift-ed up, has lift-ed up the low-ly.

Psalm tone

⁴⁷My soul proclaims the greatness óf the Lord;*
my spirit rejoices in Ǵod my Savior,
   ⁴⁸for he has l̂ooked with favor*
   on his l̂owly servant.
From this day all ǵenerations*
will ĉall me blessed;
   ⁴⁹The Almighty has done great t̂hings for me,*
   and holy ís his name. R̥
⁵⁰He has mercy on t̂hose who fear him*
in every ǵeneration.
   ⁵¹He has shown the strength óf his arm;*
   he has scattered the proud in t̂heir conceit.
⁵²He has cast down the mighty f̂rom their thrones,*
and has lifted úp the lowly.
   ⁵³He has filled the hungry ẃith good things,*
   and the rich he has sent áway empty. R̥
⁵⁴He has come to the help of his ŝervant Israel,*
for he has remembered his promíse of mercy,
   ⁵⁵the promise he made t̂o our fathers,*
   to Abraham and his child́ren forever. R̥

Alternate tone

Or, Psalm 80:1-7 (Psalter for Worship, Cycle B, p.6)

The Nativity of Our Lord (I)

Christmas Eve | Psalm 96

Refrain

Robert Hobby

4 octaves
Handbells used: 9

¹Sing to the LORD á new song;*

sing to the LORD, all t̂he whole earth.

   ²Sing to the LORD and b́less his name;*

   proclaim the good news of his salvation from d́ay to day.

³Declare his glory ám̂ong the nations*

and his wonders ám̂ong all peoples.

   ⁴For great is the LORD and greatly t́o be praised;*

   he is more to be feared t̂han all gods. ℞

⁵As for all the gods of the nations, they áre but idols;*

but it is the LORD who m̂ade the heavens.

   ⁶Oh, the majesty and magnificence óf his presence!*

   Oh, the power and the splendor of his śanctuary!

⁷Ascribe to the LORD, you families óf the peoples;*

ascribe to the LORD honór and power.

   ⁸Ascribe to the LORD the honor d́ue his name;*

   bring offerings and come int́o his courts. ℞

⁹Worship the LORD in the beaut́y of holiness;*

let the whole earth trem̂ble before him.

   ¹⁰Tell it out among the nations: "The ĹORD is king!*

   He has made the world so firm that it cannot be moved;

   he will judge the peóples with equity."

¹¹Let the heavens rejoice, and let the earth be glad;

let the sea thunder and all t̂hat is in it;*

let the field be joyful and all that ís therein.

   ¹²Then shall all the trees of the wood shout for joy

   before the LORD ẃhen he comes,*

   when he comes to ĵudge the earth.

¹³He will judge the ẃorld with righteousness*

and the peoples ẃith his truth. ℞

The Nativity of Our Lord (II)
Christmas Dawn | Psalm 97

Refrain

Robert Hobby

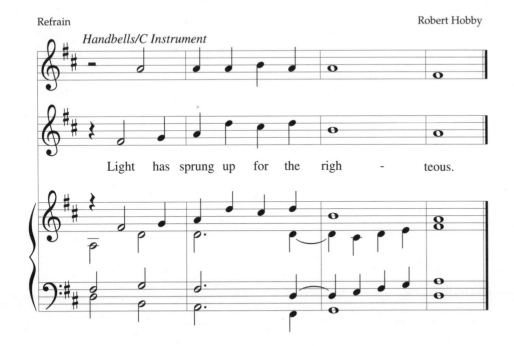

Handbells/C Instrument

Light has sprung up for the righ - teous.

[music staff]

[1]The LORD is king; let the éarth rejoice;*
let the multitude of the ísles be glad.
   [2]**Clouds and darkness are róund about him,***
   righteousness and justice are the foundations óf his throne.
[3]A fire góes before him*
and burns up his enemies on évery side.
   [4] **His lightnings light úp the world;***
   the earth sees it and ís afraid.
[5]The mountains melt like wax at the presence óf the LORD,*
at the presence of the Lord of thé whole earth.
   [6]**The heavens declare his righteousness,***
   and all the peoples sée his glory. ℟
[7]Confounded be all who worship carved images and delight ín false gods!*
Bow down before him, áll you gods.
   [8]**Zion hears and is glad, and the cities of Judáh rejoice,***
   because of your judgménts, O LORD.
[9]For you are the LORD, most high over áll the earth;*
you are exalted far abóve all gods.
   [10]**The LORD loves those whó hate evil;***
   he preserves the lives of his saints
   and delivers them from the hand óf the wicked. ℟
[11]Light has sprung up fór the righteous,*
and joyful gladness for those who áre truehearted.
   [12]**Rejoice in the LÓRD, you righteous,***
   and give thanks to his hóly name! ℟

Alternate tone

The Nativity of Our Lord (III)

Christmas Day | Psalm 98

Refrain

Robert Hobby

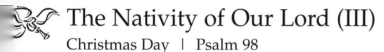

¹Sing to the LORD á new song,*
for he has done márvelous things.
　²**With his right hand and his hóly arm***
　has he won for himśelf the victory.
³The LORD has made knówn his victory;*
his righteousness has he openly shown in the sight óf the nations.
　⁴**He remembers his mercy and faithfulness to the hóuse of Israel,***
　and all the ends of the earth have seen the victory óf our God. ℟
⁵Shout with joy to the LORD, áll you lands;*
lift up your voice, rejóice, and sing.
　⁶**Sing to the LORD wíth the harp,***
　with the harp and the vóice of song.
⁷With trumpets and the sound óf the horn*
shout with joy before the kíng, the LORD.
　⁸**Let the sea make a noise and all thát is in it,***
　the lands and those who dwéll therein.
⁹Let the rivers cláp their hands,*
and let the hills ring out with joy before the LORD,
when he comes to júdge the earth.
　¹⁰**In righteousness shall he júdge the world***
　and the peóples with equity. ℟

PFW 22

First Sunday after Christmas

Psalm 148

Refrain

Robert Hobby

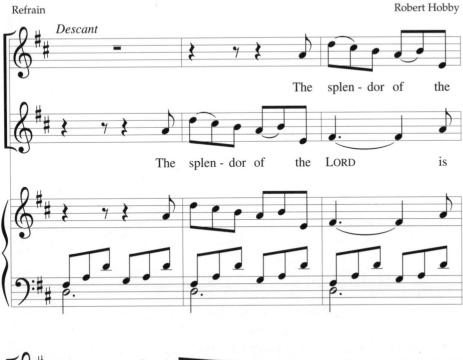

The splen-dor of the

The splen-dor of the LORD is

LORD is o - ver earth and heav'n.

o - ver earth and heav'n.

Psalm tone

¹Hallelujah! Praise the LORD from the heavens;*
praise him in the heights.
  ²Praise him, all you angels of his;*
  praise him, all his host.
³Praise him, sun and moon;*
praise him, all you shining stars.
  ⁴Praise him, heaven of heavens,*
  and you waters above the heavens.
⁵Let them praise the name of the LORD;*
for he commanded, and they were created.
  ⁶He made them stand fast forever and ever;*
  he gave them a law which shall not pass away. ℞
⁷Praise the LORD from the earth,*
you sea monsters and all deeps;
  ⁸fire and hail, snow and fog,*
  tempestuous wind, doing his will;
⁹mountains and all hills,*
fruit trees and all cedars;
  ¹⁰wild beasts and all cattle,*
  creeping things and winged birds;
¹¹kings of the earth and all peoples,*
princes and all rulers of the world;
  ¹²young men and maidens,*
  old and young together. ℞
¹³Let them praise the name of the LORD,*
for his name only is exalted, his splendor is over earth and heaven.
  ¹⁴He has raised up strength for his people and praise for all his loyal servants,*
  the children of Israel, a people who are near him. Hallelujah! ℞

Alternate tone

Second Sunday after Christmas

Psalm 147:13-21

Refrain

Robert Hobby

Lightly detached; joyfully

C Instrument

Wor - ship the LORD, O Je - ru - sa - lem;

praise your God, O Zi - on.

Psalm tone

[13]Worship the LORD, Ó Jerusalem;*
praise your Ǵod, O Zion;
 [14]**for he has strengthened the bars óf your gates;***
 he has blessed your child́ren within you.
[15]He has established peace ón your borders;*
he satisfies you with the fínest wheat.
 [16]**He sends out his command íto the earth,***
 and his word runs v́ery swiftly. R℣
[17]He gives śnow like wool;*
he scatters hoarf́rost like ashes.
 [18]**He scatters his h́ail like bread crumbs.***
 Who can stand aǵainst his cold?
[19]He sends forth his ẃord and melts them;*
he blows with his wind, and the ẃaters flow.
 [20]**He declares his ẃord to Jacob,***
 his statutes and his judǵments to Israel.
[21]He has not done so to any óther nation;*
to them he has not revealed his judgments. H́allelujah! R℣

Alternate tone

PFW 22

The Epiphany of Our Lord
Psalm 72:1-7, 10-14

Refrain

Robert Hobby

Not too fast

Finger Cymbal

All kings shall bow down be-fore him.

All kings shall bow down be-fore him.

Psalm tone

¹Give the king your justice, O God,*
and your righteousness to the king's son;
  ²that he may rule your people righteously*
  and the poor with justice;
³that the mountains may bring prosperity to the people,*
and the little hills bring righteousness.
  ⁴He shall defend the needy among the people;*
  he shall rescue the poor and crush the oppressor. ℟
⁵He shall live as long as the sun and moon endure,*
from one generation to another.
  ⁶He shall come down like rain upon the mown field,*
  like showers that water the earth.
⁷In his time shall the righteous flourish;*
there shall be abundance of peace till the moon shall be no more.
  ¹⁰The kings of Tarshish and of the isles shall pay tribute,*
  and the kings of Arabia and Saba offer gifts. ℟
¹¹All kings shall bow down before him,*
and all the nations do him service.
  ¹²For he shall deliver the poor who cries out in distress,*
  and the oppressed who has no helper.
¹³He shall have pity on the lowly and poor;*
he shall preserve the lives of the needy.
  ¹⁴He shall redeem their lives from oppression and violence,*
  and dear shall their blood be in his sight. ℟

Alternate tone

The Baptism of Our Lord

First Sunday after the Epiphany | Psalm 29

Psalm tone

Refrain

Robert Hobby

¹Ascribe to the LORD, you gods,*
ascribe to the LORD glory and strength.
   ²Ascribe to the LORD the glory due his name;*
   worship the LORD in the beauty of holiness.
³The voice of the LORD is upon the waters; the God of glory thunders;*
the LORD is upon the mighty waters.
   ⁴The voice of the LORD is a powerful voice;*
   the voice of the LORD is a voice of splendor. ℟
⁵The voice of the LORD breaks the cedar trees;*
the LORD breaks the cedars of Lebanon;
   ⁶he makes Lebanon skip like a calf,*
   and Mount Hermon like a young wild ox.
⁷The voice of the LORD splits the flames of fire;
the voice of the LORD shakes the wilderness;*
the LORD shakes the wilderness of Kadesh.
   ⁸The voice of the LORD makes the oak trees writhe*
   and strips the forests bare. ℟
⁹And in the temple of the LORD*
all are crying, "Glory!"
   ¹⁰The LORD sits enthroned above the flood;*
   the LORD sits enthroned as king forevermore.
¹¹The LORD shall give strength to his people;*
the LORD shall give his people the blessing of peace. ℟

Alternate tone

Second Sunday after the Epiphany

Psalm 36:5-10

Refrain

Daniel Kallman

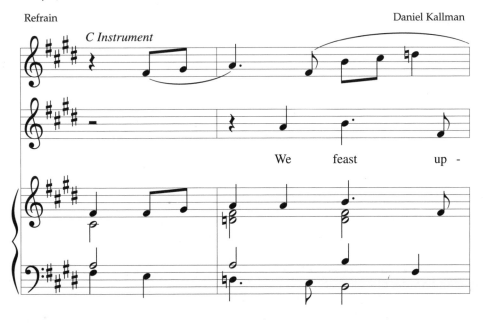

We feast up -

Psalm tone

[5]Your love, O LORD, reaches to the heavens,*
and your faithfulness to the clouds.
**[6]Your righteousness is like the strong mountains,
your justice like the great deep;***
you save both man and beast, O LORD. R̥
[7]How priceless is your love, O God!*
Your people take refuge under the shadow of your wings.
[8]They feast upon the abundance of your house;*
you give them drink from the river of your delights.
[9]For with you is the well of life,*
and in your light we see light.
[10]Continue your lovingkindness to those who know you,*
and your favor to those who are true of heart. R̥

on the a - bun - dance of your house, O LORD.

Alternate tone

The introduction may begin on the last note of the verse preceding the refrain.

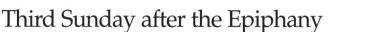

Third Sunday after the Epiphany
Psalm 19

Refrain

Daniel Kallman

The law of the LORD re - vives the soul.

[1]The heavens declare the glory of God,*
and the firmament shows his handiwork.
   [2]One day tells its tale to another,*
   and one night imparts knowledge to another.
[3]Although they have no words or language,*
and their voices are not heard,
   [4]their sound has gone out into all lands,*
   and their message to the ends of the world.
[5]In the deep has he set a pavilion for the sun;*
it comes forth like a bridegroom out of his chamber;
it rejoices like a champion to run its course.
   [6]It goes forth from the uttermost edge of the heavens
   and runs about to the end of it again;*
   nothing is hidden from its burning heat. ℟
[7]The law of the LORD is perfect and revives the soul;*
the testimony of the LORD is sure and gives wisdom to the innocent.
   [8]The statutes of the LORD are just and rejoice the heart;*
   the commandment of the LORD is clear and gives light to the eyes.
[9]The fear of the LORD is clean and endures forever;*
the judgments of the LORD are true and righteous altogether.
   [10]More to be desired are they than gold, more than much fine gold,*
   sweeter far than honey, than honey in the comb. ℟
[11]By them also is your servant enlightened,*
and in keeping them there is great reward.
   [12]Who can tell how often he offends?*
   Cleanse me from my secret faults.
[13]Above all, keep your servant from presumptuous sins;
let them not get dominion over me;*
then shall I be whole and sound, and innocent of a great offense.
   [14]Let the words of my mouth and the meditation of my heart
   be acceptable in your sight,*
   O LORD, my strength and my redeemer. ℟

Fourth Sunday after the Epiphany

Psalm 71:1-6

Refrain

Daniel Kallman

From my moth-er's womb you have been my strength.

4 octaves [3 octaves]
Handbells used: 18 [11]

opt.

Psalm tone

[1]In you, O LORD, have I taken refuge;*
let me never be ashamed.
   [2]In your righteousness, deliver me and set me free;*
   incline your ear to me and save me.
[3]Be my strong rock, a castle to keep me safe;*
you are my crag and my stronghold.
   [4]Deliver me, my God, from the hand of the wicked,*
   from the clutches of the evildoer and the oppressor. ℟
[5]For you are my hope, O Lord GOD,*
my confidence since I was young.
   [6]I have been sustained by you ever since I was born;
   from my mother's womb you have been my strength;*
   my praise shall be always of you. ℟

Alternate tone

Fifth Sunday after the Epiphany
Psalm 138

Daniel Kallman

Refrain

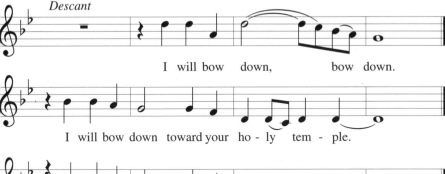

I will bow down, bow down.

I will bow down toward your ho - ly tem - ple.

[1]I will give thanks to you, O LORD, with my whole heart;*
before the gods I will sing your praise.
   [2]I will bow down toward your holy temple and praise your name,*
   because of your love and faithfulness;
[3]for you have glorified your name*
and your word above all things.
   [4]When I called, you answered me;*
   you increased my strength within me. R̥
[5]All the kings of the earth will praise you, O LORD,*
when they have heard the words of your mouth.
   [6]They will sing of the ways of the LORD,*
   that great is the glory of the LORD.
[7]Though the LORD be high, he cares for the lowly;*
he perceives the haughty from afar.
   [8]Though I walk in the midst of trouble, you keep me safe;*
   you stretch forth your hand against the fury of my enemies;
   your right hand shall save me.
[9]The LORD will make good his purpose for me;*
O LORD, your love endures forever;
do not abandon the works of your hands. R̥

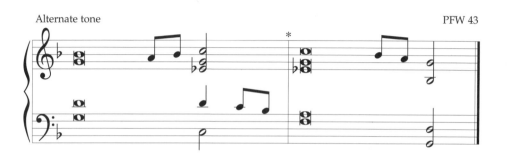

Sixth Sunday after the Epiphany

Proper 1 | Psalm 1

Refrain

Daniel Kallman

They are like trees plant-ed by streams of wa - ter. ter.

[1]Happy are they who have not walked in the counsel óf the wicked,*
nor lingered in the way of sinners, nor sat in the seats óf the scornful!
   [2]**Their delight is in the law óf the LORD,***
   and they meditate on his law day and night. Ŗ
[3]They are like trees planted by streams of water,
bearing fruit in due season, with leaves that do not wither;*
everything they do shall prosper.
   [4]**It is not so with the wicked;***
   they are like chaff which the wind blows away.
[5]Therefore the wicked shall not stand upright when judgment comes,*
nor the sinner in the council óf the righteous.
   [6]**For the LORD knows the way óf the righteous,***
   but the way of the wicked is doomed. Ŗ

Seventh Sunday after the Epiphany

Proper 2 | Psalm 37:1-12, 41-42

Refrain

Daniel Kallman

The low - ly shall pos - sess the land;

they will de-light in a - bun - dance of peace.

Psalm tone

[1]Do not fret yourself because of évildoers;*
do not be jealous of those who do wrong.
[2]For they shall soon wither líke the grass,*
and like the green grass fáde away.
[3]Put your trust in the LORD ánd do good;*
dwell in the land and feed ón its riches.
[4]Take delight ín the LORD,*
and he shall give you your héart's desire. ℟
[5]Commit your way to the LORD and put your trust in him,*
and he will bring ít to pass.
[6]He will make your righteousness as clear ás the light*
and your just dealing ás the noonday.
[7]Be still before the LORD*
and wait patiently for him.
[8]Do not fret yourself over the óne who prospers,*
the one who succeeds in évil schemes.
[9]Refrain from anger, leave ráge alone;*
do not fret yourself; it leads onlý to evil.
[10]For evildoers shall bé cut off,*
but those who wait upon the LORD shall posséss the land. ℟
[11]In a little while the wicked shall bé no more;*
you shall search out their place, but they will nót be there.
[12]But the lowly shall posséss the land;*
they will delight in abundánce of peace.
[41]But the deliverance of the righteous comes from the LORD;*
he is their stronghold in tíme of trouble.
[42]The LORD will help them and réscue them;*
he will rescue them from the wicked and deliver them,
because they seek refúge in him. ℟

Alternate tone

Eighth Sunday after the Epiphany
Proper 3 | Psalm 92:1-4, 11-14

Refrain

Daniel Kallman

The righ-teous shall flour-ish like a palm tree.

Psalm tone

[1] It is a good thing to give thanks îo the LORD,*
and to sing praises to your name, Ó Most High;

[2] to tell of your lovingkindness early în the morning*
and of your faithfulness in the night season;

[3] on the psaltery, and ón the lyre,*
and to the melody óf the harp.

[4] For you have made me glad by your ácts, O LORD;*
and I shout for joy because of the works óf your hands. R

[11] The righteous shall flourish lîke a palm tree,*
and shall spread abroad like a cedar of Lebanon.

[12] Those who are planted in the house óf the LORD*
shall flourish in the courts óf our God;

[13] they shall still bear fruit în old age;*
they shall be green and succulent;

[14] that they may show how upríght the LORD is,*
my rock, in whom there îs no fault. R

Alternate tone

PFW 43

The Transfiguration of Our Lord
Last Sunday after the Epiphany | Psalm 99

Refrain

Martin Seltz

Psalm tone

Pro - claim the great - ness of the LORD;

wor - ship up - on God's ho - ly hill.

[1]The LORD is king; let the people tremble.*
He is enthroned upon the cherubim; let the earth shake.
   [2]The LORD is great in Zion;*
   he is high above all peoples.
[3]Let them confess his name, which is great and awesome;*
he is the Holy One.
   [4]"O mighty King, lover of justice, you have established equity;*
   you have executed justice and righteousness in Jacob." R
[5]Proclaim the greatness of the LORD our God and fall down before his footstool;*
he is the Holy One.
   [6]Moses and Aaron among his priests,
   and Samuel among those who call upon his name,*
   they called upon the LORD, and he answered them.
[7]He spoke to them out of the pillar of cloud;*
they kept his testimonies and the decree that he gave them.
   [8]O LORD our God, you answered them indeed;*
   you were a God who forgave them, yet punished them for their evil deeds.
[9]Proclaim the greatness of the LORD our God and worship him upon his holy hill;*
for the LORD our God is the Holy One. R

Alternate tone

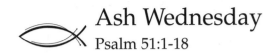

Ash Wednesday
Psalm 51:1-18

Refrain

May Schwarz

Have mer - cy on me, O God, ac - cord-ing to your lov - ing - kind- ness.

Descants for C Instrument

A

B

C

D

E

This setting of Psalm 51:1 lends itself to a variety of applications:

—It may be sung in the customary way as the psalm refrain where indicated.

—It may be sung in unison or in harmony, accompanied or unaccompanied.

—During the imposition of ashes or at another point in the Ash Wednesday liturgy, it may be used independently as a repeated refrain. It may be sung in succession as few as two or three times, as many as twenty or more times (particularly if used with the descants). The repetition allows time for meditation on the text and is useful for times when worshipers are moving in procession.

—Used in this independent fashion, it may serve as a seasonal refrain for use during the communion throughout the season of Lent.

—It may be used as part of an order of confession and forgiveness, especially when such an order includes a procession to receive an individual sign of forgiveness.

The descants are intended to be played above the refrain by a flute or other treble instrument.

—When the refrain alternates with psalm verses, one or more of the descants may be selected.

—When the refrain is used independently as an ostinato, the descants may be used in close succession above the refrain, on every other repetition, or interspersed freely at the discretion of the performer. Additional descants may be improvised.

—It is suggested that the first descant be used as first and final descant.

¹Have mercy on me, O God, according to your lovingkindness;*
in your great compassion blot out my offenses.

    ²Wash me through and through from my wickedness,*
    and cleanse me from my sin.

³For I know my transgressions,*
and my sin is ever before me.

    ⁴Against you only have I sinned*
    and done what is evil in your sight. ℞

⁵And so you are justified when you speak*
and upright in your judgment.

    ⁶Indeed, I have been wicked from my birth,*
    a sinner from my mother's womb.

⁷For behold, you look for truth deep within me,*
and will make me understand wisdom secretly.

    ⁸Purge me from my sin, and I shall be pure;*
    wash me, and I shall be clean indeed. ℞

⁹Make me hear of joy and gladness,*
that the body you have broken may rejoice.

    ¹⁰Hide your face from my sins,*
    and blot out all my iniquities.

¹¹Create in me a clean heart, O God,*
and renew a right spirit within me.

    ¹²Cast me not away from your presence,*
    and take not your Holy Spirit from me. ℞

¹³Give me the joy of your saving help again*
and sustain me with your bountiful Spirit.

    ¹⁴I shall teach your ways to the wicked,*
    and sinners shall return to you.

¹⁵Deliver me from death, O God,*
and my tongue shall sing of your righteousness, O God of my salvation.

    ¹⁶Open my lips, O Lord,*
    and my mouth shall proclaim your praise.

¹⁷Had you desired it, I would have offered sacrifice,*
but you take no delight in burnt-offerings.

    ¹⁸The sacrifice of God is a troubled spirit;*
    a broken and contrite heart, O God, you will not despise. ℞

First Sunday in Lent
Psalm 91:1-2, 9-16

Thomas Keesecker

Refrain

C Instrument

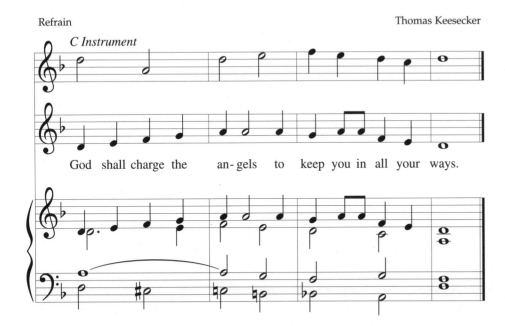

God shall charge the an-gels to keep you in all your ways.

[1]He who dwells in the shelter of the Most High,*
abides under the shadow of the Almighty.
> **[2]He shall say to the LORD, "You are my refuge and my stronghold,***
> **my God in whom I put my trust." R̥**

[9]Because you have made the LORD your refuge,*
and the Most High your habitation,
> **[10]there shall no evil happen to you,***
> **neither shall any plague come near your dwelling.**

[11]For he shall give his angels charge over you,*
to keep you in all your ways.
> **[12]They shall bear you in their hands,***
> **lest you dash your foot against a stone. R̥**

[13]You shall tread upon the lion and the adder;*
you shall trample the young lion and the serpent under your feet.
> **[14]Because he is bound to me in love, therefore will I deliver him;***
> **I will protect him, because he knows my name.**

[15]He shall call upon me, and I will answer him;*
I am with him in trouble; I will rescue him and bring him to honor.
> **[16]With long life will I satisfy him,***
> **and show him my salvation. R̥**

Second Sunday in Lent
Psalm 27

Refrain

Thomas Keesecker

In the day of trou-ble, the LORD shall keep me safe.

In the day of trou-ble, the LORD shall keep me safe.

Alternate tone

PFW 45

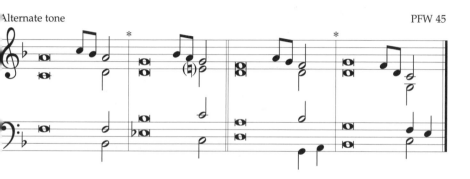

¹The LORD is my light and my salvation; whom then shall I fear?*
The LORD is the strength of my life; of whom then shall I be afraid?
   ²When evildoers came upon me to eat úp my flesh,*
   it was they, my foes and my adversaries, who stumbled and fell.
³Though an army should encamp against me,*
yet my heart shall not be afraid;
   ⁴and though war should rise úp against me,*
   yet will I put my trust in him. ℞
⁵One thing have I asked of the LORD; one thing I seek;*
that I may dwell in the house of the LORD all the days óf my life;
   ⁶to behold the fair beauty óf the LORD*
   and to seek him in his temple.
⁷For in the day of trouble he shall keep me safe in his shelter;*
he shall hide me in the secrecy of his dwelling and set me high upón a rock.
   ⁸Even now he lifts úp my head*
   above my enemies round about me. ℞
⁹Therefore I will offer in his dwelling an oblation with sounds óf great gladness;*
I will sing and make music to the LORD.
   ¹⁰Hearken to my voice, O LORD, when I call;*
   have mercy on me and ánswer me.
¹¹You speak in my heart and say, "Seek my face."*
Your face, LORD, will I seek.
   ¹²Hide not your face from me,*
   nor turn away your servant in displeasure. ℞
¹³You have been my helper; cast me not away;*
do not forsake me, O God of my salvation.
   ¹⁴Though my father and my mothér forsake me,*
   the LORD will sustain me.
¹⁵Show me your way, O LORD;*
lead me on a level path, because óf my enemies.
   ¹⁶Deliver me not into the hand of my ádversaries,*
   for false witnesses have risen up against me, and also those who speak malice.
¹⁷What if I had not believed that I should see the goodness óf the LORD*
in the land óf the living!
   ¹⁸Oh, tarry and await the LORD's pleasure;*
   be strong, and he shall comfort your heart;*
   wait patiently for the LORD. ℞

Third Sunday in Lent
Psalm 63:1-8

Refrain

Thomas Keesecker

Psalm tone

O God, ea-ger-ly I seek you; my soul thirsts for you.

[1]O God, you are my God; eagerly I seek you;*
my soul thirsts for you, my flesh faints for you,
as in a barren and dry land where there is no water.
 [2]Therefore I have gazed upon you in your holy place,*
 that I might behold your power and your glory.
[3]For your lovingkindness is better than life itself;*
my lips shall give you praise.
 [4]So will I bless you as long as I live*
 and lift up my hands in your name. Rx
[5]My soul is content, as with marrow and fatness,*
and my mouth praises you with joyful lips,
 [6]when I remember you upon my bed,*
 and meditate on you in the night watches.
[7]For you have been my helper,*
and under the shadow of your wings I will rejoice.
 [8]My soul clings to you;*
 your right hand holds me fast. Rx

Alternate tone

PFW 4

Fourth Sunday in Lent

Psalm 32

Refrain

Thomas Keesecker

I Be glad, you righ-teous, and re-joice in the LORD. II Be

glad, you righ-teous, and re-joice in the LORD.

2 octaves
Handbells used: 7

I and II *may be sung by cantor/choir and congregation, by two alternating groups within the congregation, or by all.*

Psalm tone

[1]Happy are they whose transgressions áre forgiven,*
and whose sin is p̊ut away!

   [2]Happy are they to whom the LORD imp̊utes no guilt,*
   and in whose spirit there ís no guile! R̥

[3]While I held my tongue, my bones withéred away,*
because of my groaning áll day long.

   [4]For your hand was heavy upon me d̊ay and night;*
   my moisture was dried up as in the h̊eat of summer.

[5]Then I acknowledged my śin to you,*
and did not concéal my guilt.

   [6]I said, "I will confess my transgressions t̊o the LORD."*
   Then you forgave me the guilt óf my sin.

[7]Therefore all the faithful will make their prayers to you in t̊ime of trouble;*
when the great waters overflow, they śhall not reach them.

   [8]You are my hiding-place; you preserve m̊e from trouble;*
   you surround me with shouts óf deliverance. R̥

[9]"I will instruct you and teach you in the way that ̊you should go;*
I will guide you ẘith my eye.

   [10]Do not be like horse or mule, which have no únderstanding;*
   who must be fitted with bit and bridle, or else they will ̊not stay near you."

[11]Great are the tribulations óf the wicked;*
but mercy embraces those who trust ín the LORD.

   [12]Be glad, you righteous, and rejoice ín the LORD;*
   shout for joy, all who are t̊rue of heart. R̥

Alternate tone

Fifth Sunday in Lent
Psalm 126

Refrain

Thomas Keesecker

Those who sowed with tears will

Those who sowed with tears will

To verses | Last time

reap with songs of joy. | joy.

reap with songs of joy. | joy.

Alternate accompaniment

To verses | Last time

Psalm tone

LBW 2

¹When the LORD restored the fortunes of Zion,*
then were we like those who dream.
   ²Then was our mouth filled with laughter,*
   and our tongue with shouts of joy.
³Then they said among the nations,*
"The LORD has done great things for them."
   ⁴The LORD has done great things for us,*
   and we are glad indeed. R
⁵Restore our fortunes, O LORD,*
like the watercourses of the Negev.
   ⁶Those who sowed with tears*
   will reap with songs of joy.
⁷Those who go out weeping, carrying the seed,*
will come again with joy, shouldering their sheaves. R

Alternate tone

PFW 44

Sunday of the Passion

Palm Sunday | Psalm 31:9-16

Refrain

Robert Buckley Farlee

In - to your hands, O LORD, I com - mend my spir - it.

[9]Have mercy on me, O LORD, for I ám in trouble;*
my eye is consumed with sorrow, and also my throat ánd my belly.
   [10]For my life is wasted with grief, and my ýears with sighing;*
   my strength fails me because of affliction, and my bones áre consumed.
[11]I have become a reproach to all my enemies and even to my neighbors,
a dismay to those of mý acquaintance;*
when they see me in the street they avoid me.
   [12]I am forgotten like a dead man, óut of mind;*
   I am as useless as a bróken pot. R̲
[13]For I have heard the whispering of the crowd; fear is áll around;*
they put their heads together against me; they plot to táke my life.
   [14]But as for me, I have trusted in ýou, O LORD.*
   I have said, "You áre my God.
[15]My times are ín your hand;*
rescue me from the hand of my enemies, and from those who pérsecute me.
   [16]Make your face to shine upón your servant,*
   and in your lovingkindness save me." R̲

Monday in Holy Week
Psalm 36:5-11

Refrain

Robert Buckley Farlee

Your peo - ple take ref - uge un - der the shad-ow of your wings.

[5]Your love, O Lord, reaches to the heavens,*
and your faithfulness to the clouds.
   [6]**Your righteousness is like the strong mountains,**
   your justice like the great deep;*
   you save both man and beast, O Lord.
[7]How priceless is your love, O God!*
Your people take refuge under the shadow of your wings.
   [8]**They feast upon the abundance of your house;***
   you give them drink from the river of your delights. R
[9]For with you is the well of life,*
and in your light we see light.
   [10]**Continue your lovingkindness to those who know you,***
   and your favor to those who are true of heart.
[11]Let not the foot of the proud come near me*
nor the hand of the wicked push me aside. **R**

Tuesday in Holy Week
Psalm 71:1-14

Refrain

Robert Buckley Farlee

From my moth-er's womb you have been my strength.

Alternate tone

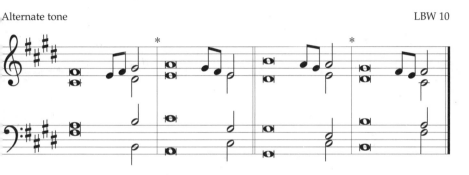

Psalm tone

¹In you, O Lord, have I taken refuge;*
let me never be ashamed.
  ²In your righteousness, deliver me and set me free;*
  incline your ear to me and save me.
³Be my strong rock, a castle to keep me safe;*
you are my crag and my stronghold.
  ⁴Deliver me, my God, from the hand of the wicked,*
  from the clutches of the evildoer and the oppressor. ℟
⁵For you are my hope, O Lord God,*
my confidence since I was young.
  ⁶I have been sustained by you ever since I was born;*
  from my mother's womb you have been my strength;*
  my praise shall be always of you.
⁷I have become a portent to many;*
but you are my refuge and my strength.
  ⁸Let my mouth be full of your praise*
  and your glory all the day long. ℟
⁹Do not cast me off in my old age;*
forsake me not when my strength fails.
  ¹⁰For my enemies are talking against me,*
  and those who lie in wait for my life take counsel together.
¹¹They say, "God has forsaken him; go after him and seize him;*
because there is none who will save."
  ¹²O God, be not far from me;*
  come quickly to help me, O my God.
¹³Let those who set themselves against me be put to shame and be disgraced;*
let those who seek to do me evil be covered with scorn and reproach.
  ¹⁴But I shall always wait in patience,*
  and shall praise you more and more. ℟

Wednesday in Holy Week
Psalm 70

Robert Buckley Farlee

Refrain

Be pleased, O God, to de-liv-er me.

[1]Be pleased, O God, to delíver me;*
O LORD, make háste to help me.

> **[2]Let those who seek my life be ashamed and altogethér dismayed;***
> **let those who take pleasure in my misfortune draw back**
> **and bé disgraced.**

[3]Let those who say to me "Aha!" and gloat over me turn back,*
because they áre ashamed.

> **[4]Let all who seek you rejoice and be glad in you;***
> **let those who love your salvation say forever, "Great ís the LORD!"** ℟

[5]But as for me, I am póor and needy;*
come to me speedíly, O God.

> **[6]You are my helper and my deliverer;***
> **O LORD, do not tarry. ℟**

Maundy Thursday
Psalm 116:1, 10-17

Refrain

Robert Buckley Farlee

I will take the cup of sal-va-tion and

call on the name of the LORD.

[1] I love the LORD, because he has heard the voice of my supplication,*
because he has inclined his ear to me whenever I called upon him.
   [10] How shall I repay the LORD*
   for all the good things he has done for me?
[11] I will lift up the cup of salvation*
and call upon the name of the LORD.
   [12] I will fulfill my vows to the LORD*
   in the presence of all his people. R
[13] Precious in the sight of the LORD*
is the death of his servants.
   [14] O LORD, I am your servant;*
   I am your servant and the child of your handmaid;
   you have freed me from my bonds.
[15] I will offer you the sacrifice of thanksgiving*
and call upon the name of the LORD.
   [16] I will fulfill my vows to the LORD*
   in the presence of all his people,
[17] in the courts of the LORD's house,*
in the midst of you, O Jerusalem. R

Alternate tone

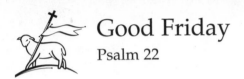

Good Friday
Psalm 22

Refrain

Robert Buckley Farlee

My God, my God, why have you for - sak - en me?

Psalm tone

LBW 2

¹My God, my God, why have you forsáken me*
and are so far from my cry, and from the words of mý distress?
  ²O my God, I cry in the daytime, but you do not answer;*
  by night as well, but I find no rest.
³Yet you are the Hóly One,*
enthroned upon the praisés of Israel.
  ⁴Our forefathers put their trust in you;*
  they trusted, and you delivered them. R̷
⁵They cried out to you and wére delivered;*
they trusted in you and were not put to shame.
  ⁶But as for me, I am a worm ánd no man,*
  scorned by all and despised by the people.
⁷All who see me laugh me to scorn;*
they curl their lips and wag their heads, saying,
  ⁸"He trusted in the LORD; let him delíver him;*
  let him rescue him, if he delights in him." R̷
⁹Yet you are he who took me out óf the womb,*
and kept me safe upon my mother's breast.

¹⁰I have been entrusted to you ever since Í was born;*
you were my God when I was still in my mother's womb.
¹¹Be not far from me, for trouble is near,*
and there is none to help.
  ¹²Many young bulls encircle me;*
  strong bulls of Bashan surround me. R̷
¹³They open wide their jaws at me,*
like a ravening and a roaring lion.
  ¹⁴I am poured out like water; all my bones are óut of joint;*
  my heart within my breast is melting wax.
¹⁵My mouth is dried out like a pot-sherd;*
my tongue sticks to the roof óf my mouth;*
and you have laid me in the dust óf the grave.
  ¹⁶Packs of dogs close me in, and gangs of evildoers circle around me;*
  they pierce my hands and my feet, I can count áll my bones. R̷
¹⁷They stare and gloat óver me;*
they divide my garments among them; they cast lots for my clothing.
  ¹⁸Be not far awáy, O LORD;*
  you are my strength; hastén to help me.
¹⁹Save me from the sword,*
my life from the power óf the dog.
  ²⁰Save me from the líon's mouth,*
  my wretched body from the horns óf wild bulls. R̷
²¹I will declare your name ío my brethren;*
in the midst of the congregation Í will praise you.
  ²²Praise the LORD, ýou that fear him;*
  stand in awe of him, O offspring of Israel; all you of Jacob's líne, give glory.
²³For he does not despise nor abhor the poor in their poverty;*
neither does he hide his fáce from them;*
but when they cry to him he hears them.
  ²⁴My praise is of him in the great assembly;*
  I will perform my vows in the presence of those who worship him. R̷
²⁵The poor shall eat and be satisfied,*
and those who seek the LORD shall praise him:*
"May your heart líve forever!"
  ²⁶All the ends of the earth shall remember and turn ío the LORD,*
  and all the families of the nations shall bow before him.
²⁷For kingship belongs ío the LORD;*
he rules óver the nations.
  ²⁸To him alone all who sleep in the earth bow dówn in worship;*
  all who go down to the dust fáll before him.
²⁹My soul shall live for him; my descendants shall serve him;*
they shall be known as the LORD's forever.
  ³⁰They shall come and make known to a people ýet unborn*
  the saving deeds that he has done. R̷

Alternate tone

PFW 25

Vigil of Easter

Response 1 | Psalm 136:1-9, 23-26

Thomas Pavlechko

Refrain

Psalm tone

God's mer - cy en - dures for - ev - er.

God's mer - cy en - dures for - ev - er.

Last time

¹Give thanks to the LORD, for he is good,*
for his mercy endures forever.
   ²**Give thanks to the God of gods,***
   for his mercy endures forever.
³Give thanks to the Lord of lords,*
for his mercy endures forever;
   ⁴**who only does great wonders,***
   for his mercy endures forever;
⁵who by wisdom made the heavens,*
for his mercy endures forever;
   ⁶**who spread out the earth upon the waters,***
   for his mercy endures forever; ℞
⁷who created great lights,*
for his mercy endures forever;
   ⁸**the sun to rule the day,***
   for his mercy endures forever;
⁹the moon and the stars to govern the night,*
for his mercy endures forever;
   ²³**who remembered us in our low estate,***
   for his mercy endures forever;
²⁴and delivered us from our enemies,*
for his mercy endures forever;
   ²⁵**who gives food to all creatures,***
   for his mercy endures forever.
²⁶Give thanks to the God of heaven,*
for his mercy endures forever. ℞

Each Vigil response includes a vocal harmony version, for use especially when these responses are sung unaccompanied. See pp. 126-129 for reproducible melody and harmony versions of these refrains.

Vigil of Easter
Response 2 | Psalm 46

Refrain

Dale Wood

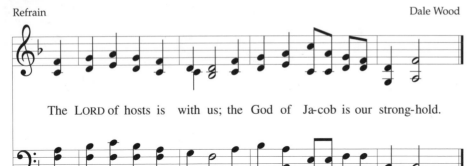

The LORD of hosts is with us; the God of Ja-cob is our strong-hold.

Alternate accompaniment

Descant

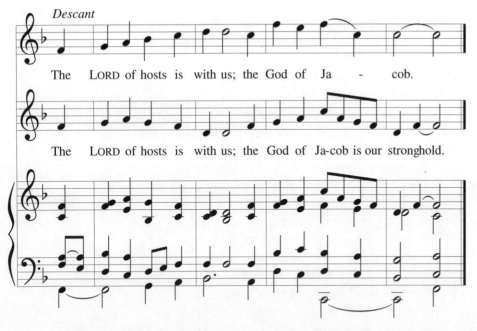

The LORD of hosts is with us; the God of Ja - cob.

The LORD of hosts is with us; the God of Ja-cob is our stronghold.

Psalm tone

¹God is our refúge and strength,*
a very present hélp in trouble.
²Therefore we will not fear, though the éarth be moved,*
and though the mountains be toppled into the depths óf the sea;
³though its waters ráge and foam,*
and though the mountains tremble át its tumult.
℟ ⁴**The Lord of hosts is with us; the God of Jacob is our stronghold.**

⁵There is a river whose streams make glad the citý of God,*
the holy habitation of the Most High.
⁶God is in the midst of her; she shall not be óverthrown;*
God shall help her at the bréak of day.
⁷The nations make much ado, and the kingdoms are shaken;*
God has spoken, and the earth shall mélt away.
℟ ⁸**The Lord of hosts is with us; the God of Jacob is our stronghold.**

⁹Come now and look upon the works óf the LORD,*
what awesome things he has dóne on earth.
¹⁰It is he who makes war to cease in áll the world;*
he breaks the bow, and shatters the spear,
and burns the shields with fire.
¹¹"Be still, then, and know that Í am God;*
I will be exalted among the nations; I will be exalted ín the earth."
℟ ¹²**The Lord of hosts is with us; the God of Jacob is our stronghold.**

In this setting of Psalm 46, all verses are sung by cantor or choir; the congregation may join in singing the above refrain, which occurs at verses 4, 8, and 12. For another method of singing this psalm, see Reformation Day, p. 118.

Vigil of Easter
Response 3 | Psalm 16

Refrain

May Schwarz

C Instrument descants

A

B

C

D

You will show me the path of life.

You will show me the path of life.

Psalm tone

*

[1]Protect me, O God, for I take refúge in you;*
I have said to the LORD, "You are my Lord, my good abóve all other."
  [2]All my delight is upon the godly that are ín the land,*
  upon those who are noble amóng the people.
[3]But those who run after óther gods*
shall have their troubles múltiplied.
  [4]Their libations of blood I wíll not offer,*
  nor take the names of their gods upón my lips. R
[5]O LORD, you are my portion ánd my cup;*
it is you who uphóld my lot.
  [6]My boundaries enclose a pléasant land;*
  indeed, I have a góodly heritage.
[7]I will bless the LORD who gíves me counsel;*
my heart teaches me night áfter night.
  [8]I have set the LORD alwáys before me;*
  because he is at my right hand, I shall not fall. R
[9]My heart, therefore, is glad, and my spirít rejoices;*
my body also shall rést in hope.
  [10]For you will not abandon me to the grave,*
  nor let your holy one sée the pit.
[11]You will show me the páth of life;*
in your presence there is fullness of joy,
and in your right hand are pleasures forévermore. R

Vigil of Easter

Response 4 | Exodus 15:1b-13, 17-18

Refrain

Mark Sedio

I will sing to the LORD who has tri - umphed glo - rious - ly.

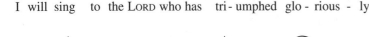

I will sing to the LORD who has tri - umphed glo - rious - ly.

[1b]I will sing to the LORD, for he has triumphed gloriously;*
horse and rider he has thrown into the sea.
[2]The Lord is my strength and my might,*
and he has become my salvation;
> this is my God, and I will praise him,*
> my father's God, and I will exalt him.
> [3]The LORD is a warrior;*
> the LORD is his name. R

[4]Pharaoh's chariots and his army he cast into the sea;*
his picked officers were sunk in the Red Sea.
[5]The floods covered them;*
they went down into the depths like a stone.
> [6]Your right hand, O LORD, glorious in power—*
> your right hand, O LORD, shattered the enemy.
> [7]In the greatness of your majesty you overthrew your adversaries;*
> you sent out your fury, it consumed them like stubble. R

[8]At the blast of your nostrils the waters piled up, the floods stood up in a heap;
the deeps congealed in the heart of the sea.
[9]The enemy said, 'I will pursue, I will overtake,
I will divide the spoil, my desire shall have its fill of them.*
I will draw my sword, my hand shall destroy them.
> [10]You blew with your wind, the sea covered them;*
> they sank like lead in the mighty waters.
> [11]Who is like you, O LORD, among the gods?*
> Who is like you, majestic in holiness,
> awesome in splendor, doing wonders? R

[12]You stretched out your right hand,*
the earth swallowed them.
[13]In your steadfast love you led the people whom you redeemed;*
you guided them by your strength to your holy abode.
> [17]You brought them in and planted them
> on the mountain of your own possession,*
> the place, O LORD, that you made your abode,
> the sanctuary, O LORD, that your hands have established.*
> [18]The LORD will reign forever and ever. R

Vigil of Easter

Response 5 | Isaiah 12:2-6

Refrain

Robert Buckley Farlee

With joy you will draw

With joy you will draw

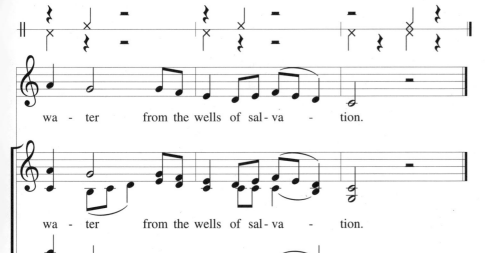

wa - ter from the wells of sal - va - tion.

wa - ter from the wells of sal - va - tion.

Psalm tone

²Surely God is my salvation;*
I will trust, and will not be afraid,
    for the Lord God is my strength ánd my might;*
    he has become my salvation. ℟
³With joy you will draw water*
from the wells óf salvation.
    ⁴And you will say ín that day:*
    Give thanks to the Lord, call ón his name;
make known his deeds amóng the nations;
proclaim that his name ís exalted.
    ⁵Sing praises to the Lord, for he hás done gloriously;
    let this be known in áll the earth.
⁶Shout aloud and sing for joy, O róyal Zion,
for great in your midst is the Holy Óne of Israel. ℟

Vigil of Easter

Response 6 | Psalm 19

May Schwarz

Refrain

The stat - utes of the LORD are ... just and re - joice the heart.

The stat - utes of the LORD are ... just and re - joice the heart.

The heavens declare the glory of God,*
and the firmament shows his handiwork.
One day tells its tale to another,*
and one night imparts knowledge to another.
   ³Although they have no words or language,*
   and their voices áre not heard,
   ⁴their sound has gone out into all lands,*
   and their message to the ends óf the world. ℞
In the deep has he set a pavilion for the sun;*
it comes forth like a bridegroom out of his chamber;
it rejoices like a champion to run its course.
It goes forth from the uttermost edge of the heavens
and runs about to the end of it again;*
nothing is hidden from its burning heat.
   ⁷The law of the Lᴏʀᴅ is perfect and revives the soul;*
   the testimony of the Lᴏʀᴅ is sure and gives wisdom to the innocent.
   ⁸The statutes of the Lᴏʀᴅ are just and rejoice the heart;*
   the commandment of the Lᴏʀᴅ is clear and gives light to the eyes. ℞
The fear of the Lᴏʀᴅ is clean and endures forever;*
the judgments of the Lᴏʀᴅ are true and righteous áltogether.
More to be desired are they than gold, more than much fine gold,*
sweeter far than honey, than honey in the comb.
   ¹¹By them also is your servant enlightened,*
   and in keeping them there is great reward.
   ¹²Who can tell how often he offends?*
   Cleanse me from my secret faults.
Above all, keep your servant from presumptuous sins;
let them not get dominion óver me;*
then shall I be whole and sound, and innocent of a great offense.
Let the words of my mouth and the meditation of my heart
be acceptable in your sight,*
O Lᴏʀᴅ, my strength and my redeemer. ℞

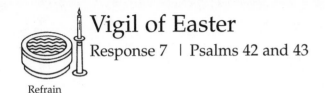

Vigil of Easter
Response 7 | Psalms 42 and 43

Mark Sedio

Refrain

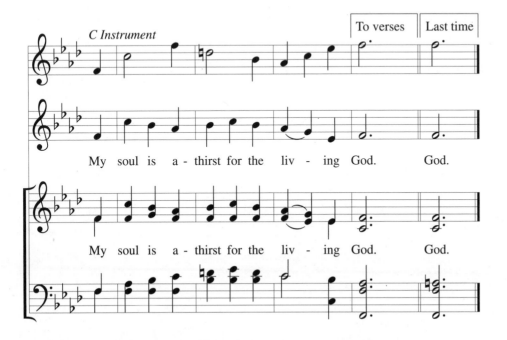

C Instrument

To verses | Last time

My soul is a- thirst for the liv - ing God. God.

My soul is a- thirst for the liv - ing God. God.

Psalm tone

PFW 47

[1]As the deer longs for the water-brooks,*
so longs my soul for you, O God.
[2]My soul is athirst for God, athirst for the living God;*
when shall I come to appear before the presence of God?
[3]My tears have been my food day and night,*
while all day long they say to me, "Where now is your God?"
[4]I pour out my soul when I think on these things;*
how I went with the multitude and led them into the house of God,
[5]with the voice of praise and thanksgiving,*
among those who keep holy-day.
[6]Why are you so full of heaviness, O my soul?*
And why are you so disquieted within me?
[7]Put your trust in God;*
for I will yet give thanks to him,
who is the help of my countenance, and my God.
[8]My soul is heavy within me;*
therefore I will remember you from the land of Jordan,
and from the peak of Mizar among the heights of Hermon. ℟
[9]One deep calls to another in the noise of your cataracts;*
all your rapids and floods have gone over me.
[10]The LORD grants his lovingkindness in the daytime;*
in the night season his song is with me, a prayer to the God of my life.
[11]I will say to the God of my strength, "Why have you forgotten me,*
and why do I go so heavily while the enemy oppresses me?"
[12]While my bones are being broken,*
my enemies mock me to my face;
[13]all day long they mock me*
and say to me, "Where now is your God?"
[14]Why are you so full of heaviness, O my soul?*
And why are you so disquieted within me?
[15]Put your trust in God;*
for I will yet give thanks to him,
who is the help of my countenance, and my God.
[1]Give judgment for me, O God, and defend my cause against an ungodly people;*
deliver me from the deceitful and the wicked. ℟
[2]For you are the God of my strength; why have you put me from you,*
and why do I go so heavily while the enemy oppresses me?
[3]Send out your light and your truth, that they may lead me,*
and bring me to your holy hill and to your dwelling;
[4]that I may go to the altar of God, to the God of my joy and gladness;*
and on the harp I will give thanks to you, O God my God.
[5]Why are you so full of heaviness, O my soul?*
And why are you so disquieted within me?
[6]Put your trust in God;*
for I will yet give thanks to him,
who is the help of my countenance and my God. ℟

Vigil of Easter
Response 8 | Psalm 143

Refrain

May Schwarz

Re - vive me, O Lord, for your name's sake.

Re - vive me, O Lord, for your name's sake.

[1]Lord, hear my prayer, and in your faithfulness heed my supplications;*
answer me in your righteousness.

   [2]**Enter not into judgment with your servant,***
   for in your sight shall no one living be justified.

[3]For my enemy has sought my life; he has crushed me to the ground;*
he has made me live in dark places like those who are long dead.

   [4]**My spirit faints within me;***
   my heart within me is desolate. R

[5]I remember the time past; I muse upon all your deeds;*
I consider the works of your hands.

   [6]**I spread out my hands to you;***
   my soul gasps to you like a thirsty land.

[7]O Lord, make haste to answer me; my spirit fails me;*
do not hide your face from me or I shall be like those who go down to the pit.

   [8]**Let me hear of your lovingkindness in the morning, for I put my trust in you;***
   show me the road that I must walk, for I lift up my soul to you. R

[9]Deliver me from my enemies, O Lord,*
for I flee to you for refuge.

   [10]**Teach me to do what pleases you, for you are my God;***
   let your good Spirit lead me on level ground.

[11]Revive me, O Lord, for your name's sake;*
for your righteousness' sake, bring me out of trouble.

   [12]**Of your goodness, destroy my enemies and bring all my foes to naught,***
   for truly I am your servant. R

Vigil of Easter

Response 9 | Psalm 98

Refrain

Mark Sedio

Psalm tone

Lift up your voice, re - joice and sing.

2 octaves
Handbells used: 7

[1]Sing to the LORD a new song,*
for he has done marvelous things.
   [2]With his right hand and his holy arm*
   has he won for himself the victory. ℟
[3]The LORD has made known his victory;*
his righteousness has he openly shown in the sight of the nations.
   [4]He remembers his mercy and faithfulness to the house of Israel,*
   and all the ends of the earth have seen the victory of our God.
[5]Shout with joy to the LORD, all you lands;*
lift up your voice, rejoice, and sing.
   [6]Sing to the LORD with the harp,*
   with the harp and the voice of song. ℟
[7]With trumpets and the sound of the horn*
shout with joy before the king, the LORD.
   [8]Let the sea make a noise and all that is in it,*
   the lands and those who dwell therein.
[9]Let the rivers clap their hands,*
and let the hills ring out with joy before the LORD,
when he comes to judge the earth.
   [10]In righteousness shall he judge the world*
   and the peoples with equity. ℟

Vigil of Easter
Response 10 | Jonah 2:1-3 [4-6] 7-9

Refrain

Robert Buckley Farlee

Psalm tone

A rainstick may be turned as the introduction (or the antiphon itself) begins.

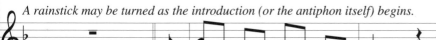

De - liv-'rance be-longs to the LORD.

optional introduction

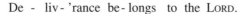

De - liv-'rance be-longs to the LORD.

²I called to the LORD out of my distress
and he ánswered me:*
out of the belly of Sheol I cried,
and you héard my voice.

> ³**You cast me into the deep, into the heart of the seas,**
> **and the flood surróunded me;***
> **all your waves and your billows**
> **passed óver me. ℟**

⁴[Then I said, 'I am driven away fróm your sight;
how shall I look again upon your hóly temple?'

> ⁵**The waters closed in over me; the deep surróunded me;***
> **weeds were wrapped around my head**
> **at the roots óf the mountains.**

⁶I went down to the land whose bars closed upon me forever;*
yet you brought up my life from the Pit, O LORD my God.]

> ⁷**As my life was ebbing away, I remémbered the LORD;***
> **and my prayer came to you, into your hóly temple.**

⁸Those who worship vain idols
forsake their true loyalty.

> ⁹**But I with the voice of thanksgiving will sacrifice to you;**
> **what I have vowed I will pay. Deliverance belongs ío the LORD! ℟**

Vigil of Easter

Response 11 | Deuteronomy 32:1-4, 7, 36a, 43a

Refrain

George W. Warren, arr. May Schwarz

Great is our God, the Rock, whose ways are just.

Great is our God, the Rock, whose ways are just.

¹Give ear to what I say, you heavens,*
and let the earth hear the words óf my mouth.
   ²My teaching shall fall like drops of rain;*
   my words shall distill ás the dew,
like fine rain upón the grass*
and like the showers ón young plants.
   ³When I call aloud in the name óf the LORD,*
   you shall respond, "Great ís our God,
⁴the rock whose work is perfect,*
and all his ways are just;
   a faithful God, who does no wrong,*
   righteous and true is he." ℟
⁷Remember the days of old:*
think of the generations long ago;
   ask your father to recount it*
   and your elders to tell you the tale.
³⁶ᵃThe LORD will give his people justice*
and have compassion ón his servants.
   ⁴³ᵃRejoice with him, you heavens:*
   all you gods, bow down before him. ℟

Vigil of Easter

Response 12 | Song of the Three Young Men 35-65

Refrain

Mark Sedio

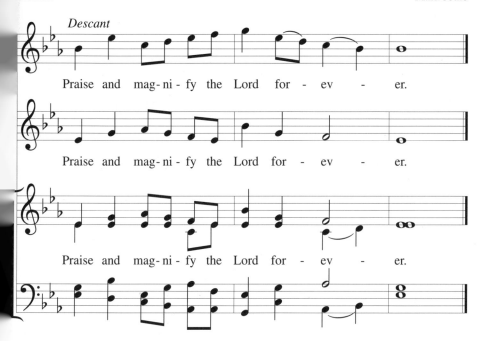

Praise and mag-ni-fy the Lord for - ev - er.

Praise and mag-ni-fy the Lord for - ev - er.

Praise and mag-ni-fy the Lord for - ev - er.

Psalm tone

PFW 48

The structure of this response calls for a three-part tone. The refrain occurs after the first verse (sung to the first part of the tone), then every three verses thereafter.

All you works of the Lord, bless the Lord—**R**

You angels of the Lord, bless the Lord;*
you heavens, bless the Lord;*
all you powers of the Lord, bless the Lord—**R**

You sun and moon, bless the Lord;*
you stars of heaven, bless the Lord;*
you showers and dews, bless the Lord—**R**

You winds of God, bless the Lord;*
you fire and heat, bless the Lord;*
you winter and summer, bless the Lord—**R**

You dews and frost, bless the Lord;*
you frost and cold, bless the Lord;*
you ice and snow, bless the Lord—**R**

You nights and days, bless the Lord;*
you light and darkness, bless the Lord; *
you lightnings and clouds, bless the Lord—**R**

Let the earth bless the Lord:*
you mountains and hills, bless the Lord;*
all you green things that grow on the earth, bless the Lord—**R**

You wells and springs, bless the Lord;*
you rivers and seas, bless the Lord;*
you whales and all who move in the waters, bless the Lord;—**R**

All you birds of the air, bless the Lord;*
all you beasts and cattle, bless the Lord;*
all you children of mortals, bless the Lord—**R**

You people of God, bless the Lord;*
you priests of the Lord, bless the Lord;*
you servants of the Lord, bless the Lord—**R**

You spirits and souls of the righteous, bless the Lord:*
you pure and humble of heart, bless the Lord;*
let us bless the Father and the Son and the Holy Spirit—**R**

Vigil of Easter

Response to the New Testament reading | Psalm 114

Robert Buckley Farlee

Refrain

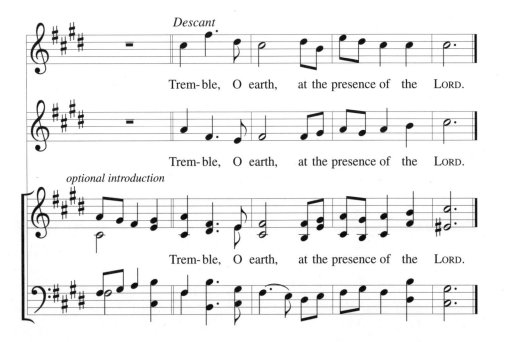

Descant

Trem-ble, O earth, at the presence of the LORD.

Trem-ble, O earth, at the presence of the LORD.

optional introduction

Trem-ble, O earth, at the presence of the LORD.

Psalm tone

[1]Hallelujah! When Israel came óut of Egypt,*
the house of Jacob from a people óf strange speech,
   [2]Judah became God's śanctuary*
   and Israel hís dominion.
[3]The sea beheld ît and fled;*
Jordan turned ánd went back.
   [4]The mountains śkipped like rams,*
   and the little hills lîke young sheep. R℣
[5]What ailed you, O sea, thât you fled,*
O Jordan, that ýou turned back,
   [6]you mountains, that you śkipped like rams,*
   you little hills lîke young sheep?
[7]Tremble, O earth, at the presence óf the LORD,*
at the presence of the Ĝod of Jacob,
   [8]who turned the hard rock into a póol of water*
   and flint-stone into a flôwing spring. R℣

The Resurrection of Our Lord

Easter Day | Psalm 118:1-2, 14-24

Refrain

Carl Schalk

2 octaves
Handbells used: 8

[1]Give thanks to the LORD, for he is good;*
his mercy endures forever.
   [2]Let Israel now proclaim,
   "His mercy endures forever."
[14]The LORD is my strength and my song,*
and he has become my salvation.
   [15]There is a sound of exultation and victory*
   in the tents of the righteous:
[16]"The right hand of the Lord has triumphed!*
The right hand of the LORD is exalted!
The right hand of the LORD has triumphed!"
   [17]I shall not die, but live,*
   and declare the works of the LORD. ℟
[18]The LORD has punished me sorely,*
but he did not hand me over to death.
   [19]Open for me the gates of righteousness;*
   I will enter them; I will offer thanks to the LORD.
[20]"This is the gate of the LORD;*
he who is righteous may enter."
   [21]I will give thanks to you, for you answered me*
   and have become my salvation. ℟
[22]The same stone which the builders rejected*
has become the chief cornerstone.
   [23]This is the LORD's doing,*
   and it is marvelous in our eyes.
[24]On this day the LORD has acted;*
we will rejoice and be glad in it. ℟

Alternate tone

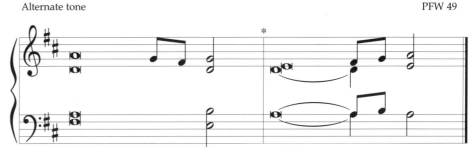

Second Sunday of Easter
Psalm 150

Refrain

Carl Schalk

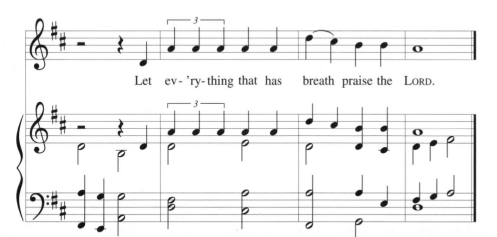

Let ev-'ry-thing that has breath praise the LORD.

Psalm tone

[1]Hallelujah! Praise God in his hóly temple;*
praise him in the firmament óf his power.
   [2]Praise him for his míghty acts;*
   praise him for his exćellent greatness. ℟
[3]Praise him with the blast óf the ram's horn;*
praise him with lýre and harp.
   [4]Praise him with timbrel and dance;*
   praise him with strings and pipe.
[5]Praise him with resóunding cymbals;*
praise him with loud-clanging cymbals.
   [6]Let everything that has breath*
   praise the LORD. Hallelujah! ℟

Alternate tone

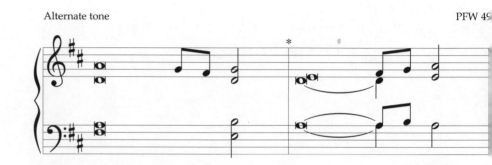

Third Sunday of Easter

Psalm 30

Refrain

Carl Schalk

Psalm tone

¹I will exalt you, O Lᴏʀᴅ, because you have liftéd me up*
and have not let my enemies triumph óver me.
  ²O Lᴏʀᴅ my God, I cried óut to you,*
  and you restored me to health.
³You brought me up, O Lᴏʀᴅ, from the dead;*
you restored my life as I was going down to the grave.
  ⁴Sing to the Lᴏʀᴅ, you servants of his;*
  give thanks for the remembrance óf his holiness.
⁵For his wrath endures but the twinkling óf an eye,*
his favor for a lifetime.
  ⁶Weeping may spend the night,*
  but joy comes in the morning. ℟
⁷While I felt secure, I said, "I shall never be disturbed.*
You, Lᴏʀᴅ, with your favor, made me as strong ás the mountains."
  ⁸Then you hid your face,*
  and I was filled with fear.
⁹I cried to you, O Lᴏʀᴅ;*
I pleaded with the Lord, saying,
  ¹⁰"What profit is there in my blood, if I go down to the pit?*
  Will the dust praise you or declare your faithfulness? ℟
¹¹Hear, O Lᴏʀᴅ, and have mercy upon me;*
O Lᴏʀᴅ, be my helper."
  ¹²You have turned my wailing ínto dancing;*
  you have put off my sackcloth and clothed me with joy.
¹³Therefore my heart sings to you without ceasing;*
O Lᴏʀᴅ my God, I will give you thanks forever. ℟

Alternate tone

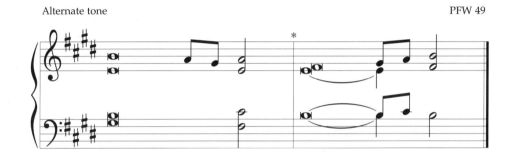

Fourth Sunday of Easter
Psalm 23

Refrain

Carl Schalk

The LORD is my shepherd; I shall not be in want.

Psalm tone

[1]The LORD is my shepherd;*
I shall not be in want.
    [2]He makes me lie down in green pastures*
    and leads me beside still waters.
[3]He revives my soul*
and guides me along right pathways for his name's sake.
    [4]Though I walk through the valley of the shadow of death,
    I shall fear no evil;*
    for you are with me; your rod and your staff, they comfort me. ℟
[5]You spread a table before me
in the presence of those who trouble me;*
you have anointed my head with oil, and my cup is running over.
    [6]Surely your goodness and mercy shall follow me
    all the days of my life,*
    and I will dwell in the house of the LORD forever. ℟

Alternate tone

PFW 49

Fifth Sunday of Easter
Psalm 148

Refrain

Carl Schalk

The splendor of the LORD is o - ver earth and heav'n.

Psalm tone

Alternate tone

PFW 49

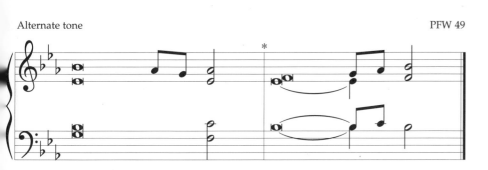

[1]Hallelujah! Praise the LORD from the heavens;*
praise him in the heights.
  [2]Praise him, all you angels of his;*
  praise him, all his host.
[3]Praise him, sun and moon;*
praise him, all you shining stars.
  [4]Praise him, heaven of heavens,*
  and you waters above the heavens.
[5]Let them praise the name of the LORD;*
for he commanded, and they were created.
  [6]He made them stand fast forever and ever;*
  he gave them a law which shall not pass away. ℞
[7]Praise the LORD from the earth,*
you sea monsters and all deeps;
  [8]fire and hail, snow and fog,*
  tempestuous wind, doing his will;
[9]mountains and all hills,*
fruit trees and all cedars;
  [10]wild beasts and all cattle,*
  creeping things and winged birds;
[11]kings of the earth and all peoples,*
princes and all rulers of the world;
  [12]young men and maidens,*
  old and young together. ℞
[13]Let them praise the name of the LORD,*
for his name only is exalted, his splendor is over earth and heaven.
  [14]He has raised up strength for his people
  and praise for all his loyal servants,*
  the children of Israel, a people who are near him. Hallelujah! ℞

Sixth Sunday of Easter
Psalm 67

Refrain

Carl Schalk

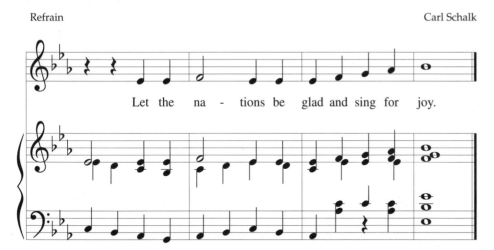

Let the na - tions be glad and sing for joy.

Psalm tone

[1]May God be merciful to ús and bless us,*
show us the light of his countenance, and ćome to us.
   [2]Let your ways be known úpon earth,*
   your saving health among all nations.
[3]Let the peoples praise ýou, O God;*
let all the ṕeoples praise you.
   [4]Let the nations be glad and śing for joy,*
   for you judge the peoples with equity
   and guide all the nations úpon earth. R̥
[5]Let the peoples praise ýou, O God;*
let all the ṕeoples praise you.
   [6]The earth has brought f́orth her increase;*
   may God, our own God, give ús his blessing.
[7]May God give ús his blessing,*
and may all the ends of the earth stand in áwe of him. **R̥**

Alternate tone

The Ascension of Our Lord
Psalm 47

Refrain

Walter Pelz

Psalm tone

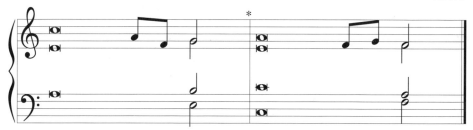

God has gone up with a shout; sing prais-es to God, sing prais- es.

[1]Clap your hands, áll you peoples;*
shout to God with a ćry of joy.
  [2]**For the LORD Most High is t́o be feared;***
  he is the great king over áll the earth.
[3]He subdues the ṕeoples under us,*
and the nations undér our feet.
  [4]**He chooses our inherítance for us,***
  the pride of Jacob ẃhom he loves.
[5]God has gone up ẃith a shout,*
the LORD with the sound óf the ram's horn.
  [6]**Sing praises to Ǵod, sing praises;***
  sing praises to our kíng, sing praises. ℞
[7]For God is king of áll the earth;*
sing praises with áll your skill.
  [8]**God reigns over the nations;***
  God sits upon his h́oly throne.
[9]The nobles of the peoples have gathéred together*
with the people of the Ǵod of Abraham.
  [10]**The rulers of the earth beĺong to God,***
  and he is highĺy exalted. ℞

Alternate tone

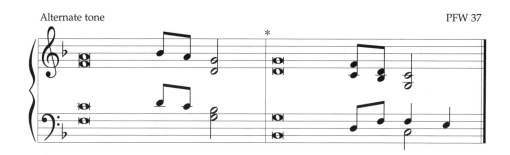

Or, Psalm 93 (see Psalter for Worship, Cycle B, p. 78).

Seventh Sunday of Easter
Psalm 97

Refrain

Carl Schalk

Descant

Re - joice in the LORD, you righ - teous.

Re - joice in the LORD, you righ - teous.

[1]The LORD is king; let the éarth rejoice;*
let the multitude of the ísles be glad.
   [2]**Clouds and darkness are found about him,***
   righteousness and justice are the foundations óf his throne.
[3]A fire goes before him*
and burns up his enemies on évery side.
   [4]**His lightnings light úp the world;***
   the earth sees it and ís afraid.
[5]The mountains melt like wax at the presence óf the LORD,*
at the presence of the Lord of the whole earth.
   [6]**The heavens declare his righteousness,***
   and all the peoples see his glory. R
[7]Confounded be all who worship carved images and delight ín false gods!*
Bow down before him, áll you gods.
   [8]**Zion hears and is glad, and the cities of Judah rejoice,***
   because of your judgments, O LORD.
[9]For you are the LORD, most high over áll the earth;*
you are exalted far above all gods.
   [10]**The LORD loves those who hate evil;***
   he preserves the lives of his saints
   and delivers them from the hand óf the wicked. R
[11]Light has sprung up for the righteous,*
and joyful gladness for those who áre truehearted.
   [12]**Rejoice in the LORD, you righteous,***
   and give thanks to his holy name. R

Alternate tone

Vigil of Pentecost
Psalm 33:12-22

Robert Buckley Farlee

frain

The LORD is our help and our shield.

optional introduction

II:

I:

Man.

Ped.

Accompaniment, last time only

II:

I:

Man.

Ped.

Psalm tone

[12]Happy is the nation whose God is the LORD!*
Happy the people he has chosen to be his own!
   [13]**The LORD looks down from heaven,***
   and beholds all the people in the world.
[14]From where he sits enthroned he turns his gaze*
on all who dwell on the earth.
   [15]**He fashions all the hearts of them***
   and understands all their works. ℞
[16]There is no king that can be saved by a mighty army;*
a strong man is not delivered by his great strength.
   [17]**The horse is a vain hope for deliverance;***
   for all its strength it cannot save.
[18]Behold, the eye of the LORD is upon those who fear him,*
on those who wait upon his love,
   [19]**to pluck their lives from death,***
   and to feed them in time of famine. ℞
[20]Our soul waits for the LORD;*
he is our help and our shield.
   [21]**Indeed, our heart rejoices in him,***
   for in his holy name we put our trust.
[22]Let your lovingkindness, O LORD, be upon us,*
as we have put our trust in you. ℞

Alternate tone

The Day of Pentecost

Psalm 104:25-35, 37

Refrain

Carl Schalk

Send forth your Spir-it and re - new the face of the earth.

Psalm tone

²⁵O LORD, how manifold áre your works!*
In wisdom you have made them all; the earth is full óf your creatures.
  ²⁶Yonder is the great and wide sea with its living things too maný to number,*
  creatures both śmall and great.
²⁷There move the ships, and there is ťhat Leviathan,*
which you have made for the śport of it.
  ²⁸All of them ĺook to you*
  to give them their food ín due season. ℞
²⁹You give it to them; they ǵather it;*
you open your hand, and they are filled ẃith good things.
  ³⁰You hide your face, and ťhey are terrified;*
  you take away their breath, and they die and return ťo their dust.
³¹You send forth your Spirit, and they áre created;*
and so you renew the face óf the earth.
  ³²May the glory of the LORD enďure forever;*
  may the LORD rejoice in áll his works. ℞
³³He looks at the earth ánd it trembles;*
he touches the mountains ánd they smoke.
  ³⁴I will sing to the LORD as long ás I live;*
  I will praise my God while I ħave my being.
³⁵May these words óf mine please him;*
I will rejoice ín the LORD.
  ³⁷Bless the LORD, Ó my soul.*
  Halĺelujah! ℞

For a setting of the alternate refrain, see Psalter for Worship, Cycle B, p. 49.

Alternate tone

The Holy Trinity

First Sunday after Pentecost | Psalm 8

Refrain

Valerie Shields

Your maj - es - ty   is praised a- bove the   heav-ens.

Psalm tone

¹O Lᴏʀᴅ our Lord,*
how exalted is your name in áll the world!
   ²Out of the mouths of inf́ants and children*
   your majesty is praised abóve the heavens. ℞
³You have set up a stronghold against your ádversaries,*
to quell the enemy and t́he avenger.
   ⁴When I consider your heavens, the work óf your fingers,*
   the moon and the stars you have set ín their courses,
⁵what is man that you should be mindf́ul of him,*
the son of man that you should śeek him out?
   ⁶You have made him but little lower t́han the angels;*
   you adorn him with glóry and honor; ℞
⁷you give him mastery over the works óf your hands;*
you put all things und́er his feet:
   ⁸all śheep and oxen,*
   even the wild beasts óf the field,
⁹the birds of the air, the fish óf the sea,*
and whatsoever walks in the paths óf the sea.
   ¹⁰O Lᴏʀᴅ our Lord,*
   how exalted is your name in áll the world! ℞

Alternate tone

Sunday between May 29 and June 4*

Proper 4 | Psalm 96:1-9

Refrain

Valerie Shields

De - clare the glo - ry of the Lord a - mong the na - tions.

2 octaves
Handbells used: 8

[1]Sing to the Lord á new song;*
sing to the Lord, all íhe whole earth.
   [2]**Sing to the Lord and bless his name;***
   proclaim the good news of his salvation from dáy to day.
[3]Declare his glory amóng the nations*
and his wonders amóng all peoples.
   [4]**For great is the Lord and greatly ío be praised;***
   he is more to be feared íhan all gods. Rₓ
[5]As for all the gods of the nations, they áre but idols;*
but it is the Lord who máde the heavens.
   [6]**Oh, the majesty and magnificence óf his presence!***
   Oh, the power and the splendor of his śanctuary!
[7]Ascribe to the Lord, you families óf the peoples;*
ascribe to the Lord honór and power.
   [8]**Ascribe to the Lord the honor dúe his name;***
   bring offerings and come ínío his courts.
[9]Worship the Lord in the beauíy of holiness;*
let the whole earth tremble before him. **Rₓ**

Alternate tone

If after Trinity Sunday

Sunday between June 5 and 11*

Proper 5 | Psalm 30

Refrain

Valerie Shields

Descant

I cried out,

My God, I cried out to you,

you re-stored me to health.

and you re-stored me to health.

Psalm tone

¹I will exalt you, O Lord, because you have lifted me up*
and have not let my enemies triumph óver me.
    ²O Lord my God, I cried óut to you,*
    and you restored me to health.
³You brought me up, O Lord, from the dead;*
you restored my life as I was going down to the grave.
    ⁴Sing to the Lord, you servants of his;*
    give thanks for the remembrance óf his holiness. ℞
⁵For his wrath endures but the twinkling óf an eye,*
his favor for a lifetime.
    ⁶Weeping may spend the night,*
    but joy comes ín the morning.
⁷While I felt secure, I said, "I shall never be disturbed.*
You, Lord, with your favor, made me as strong ás the mountains."
    ⁸Then you hid your face,*
    and I was filled with fear. ℞
⁹I cried to you, O Lord;*
I pleaded with the Lord, saying,
    ¹⁰"What profit is there in my blood, if I go down to the pit?*
    Will the dust praise you or declare your faithfulness?
¹¹Hear, O Lord, and have mercy upon me;*
O Lord, be my helper."
    ¹²You have turned my wailing into dancing;*
    you have put off my sackcloth and clothed me with joy.
¹³Therefore my heart sings to you without ceasing;*
O Lord my God, I will give you thanks forever. ℞

Alternate tone

PFW 50

* If after Trinity Sunday

Sunday between June 12 and 18*

Proper 6 | Psalm 32

Refrain

Valerie Shields

Descant

Then you for - gave my sin.

Then you for - gave me the guilt of my sin.

[1]Happy are they whose transgressions áre forgiven,*
and whose sin is pút away!

   [2]**Happy are they to whom the LORD impútes no guilt,***
   and in whose spirit there ís no guile!

[3]While I held my tongue, my bones withéred away,*
because of my groaning áll day long.

   [4]**For your hand was heavy upon me dáy and night;***
   my moisture was dried up as in the héat of summer. R

[5]Then I acknowledged my sín to you,*
and did not concéal my guilt.

   [6]**I said, "I will confess my transgressions ío the LORD."***
   Then you forgave me the guilt óf my sin.

[7]Therefore all the faithful will make their prayers to you in íme of trouble;*
when the great waters overflow, they sháll not reach them.

   [8]**You are my hiding-place; you preserve me from trouble;***
   you surround me with shouts óf deliverance. R

[9]"I will instruct you and teach you in the way that ýou should go;*
I will guide you wíth my eye.

   [10]**Do not be like horse or mule, which have no únderstanding;***
   who must be fitted with bit and bridle, or else they will not stay near you."

[11]Great are the tribulations óf the wicked;*
but mercy embraces those who trust ín the LORD.

   [12]**Be glad, you righteous, and rejoice ín the LORD;***
   shout for joy, all who are írue of heart. R

Alternate tone

PFW 5(

If after Trinity Sunday

Sunday between June 19 and 25*

Proper 7 | Psalm 22:18-27

Refrain

Valerie Shields

In the midst of the con - gre-ga - tion I will praise you.

Psalm tone

¹⁸Be not far awáy, O LORD;*
you are my strength; hastén to help me.
   ¹⁹**Save me frŏm the sword,***
   my life from the power óf the dog.
²⁰Save me from the lĭon's mouth,*
my wretched body from the horns óf wild bulls.
   ²¹**I will declare your name tŏ my brethren;***
   in the midst of the congregation Í will praise you. ℟
²²Praise the LORD, ўou that fear him;*
stand in awe of him, O offspring of Israel; all you of Jacob's lĭne, give glory.
   ²³**For he does not despise nor abhor the poor in their poverty;***
   neither does he hide his fáce from them;*
   but when they cry to hĭm he hears them.
²⁴My praise is of him in the ğreat assembly;*
I will perform my vows in the presence of those who wŏrship him.
   ²⁵**The poor shall eat and be satisfied,**
   and those who seek the LORD shall praise him:*
   "May your heart lĭve forever!" ℟
²⁶All the ends of the earth shall remember and turn tŏ the LORD,*
and all the families of the nations shall bŏw before him.
   ²⁷**For kingship belongs tŏ the LORD;***
   he rules óver the nations. ℟

Alternate tone

PFW 50

* *If after Trinity Sunday*

Sunday between June 26 and July 2
Proper 8 | Psalm 16

Refrain

Valerie Shields

I have set the LORD al - ways be-fore me.

[1]Protect me, O God, for I take refúge in you;*
I have said to the LORD, "You are my Lord, my good abóve all other."
   [2]All my delight is upon the godly that are ín the land,*
   upon those who are noble amóng the people.
[3]But those who run after óther gods*
shall have their troubles múltiplied.
   [4]Their libations of blood I wíll not offer,*
   nor take the names of their gods upón my lips. ℞
[5]O LORD, you are my portion ánd my cup;*
it is you who uphóld my lot.
   [6]My boundaries enclose a pléasant land;*
   indeed, I have a góodly heritage.
[7]I will bless the LORD who gíves me counsel;*
my heart teaches me night áfter night.
   [8]I have set the LORD alwáys before me;*
   because he is at my right hand, I shall not fall. ℞
[9]My heart, therefore, is glad, and my spirít rejoices;*
my body also shall rést in hope.
   [10]For you will not abandon me tó the grave,*
   nor let your holy one sée the pit.
[11]You will show me the páth of life;*
in your presence there is fullness of joy,
and in your right hand are pleasures forévermore. ℞

Sunday between July 17 and 23

Proper 11 | Psalm 15

Refrain

John Paradowski

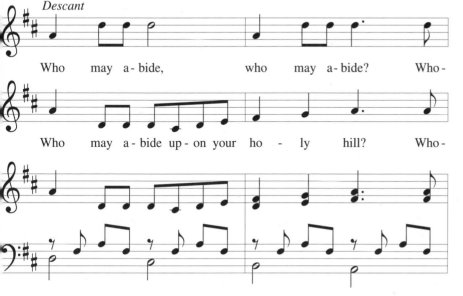

Who may a-bide, who may a-bide? Who-

Who may a-bide up-on your ho - ly hill? Who-

ev - er leads a blameless life and does what is right.

ev - er leads a blameless life and does what is right.

Psalm tone

¹Lord, who may dwell in your tabernacle?*
Who may abide upon your holy hill?
    ²Whoever leads a blameless life and does what is right,*
    who speaks the truth from his heart,
³there is no guile upon his tongue; he does no evil to his friend;*
he does not heap contempt upon his neighbor.
    ⁴In his sight the wicked is rejected,*
    but he honors those who fear the Lord. Rx
⁵He has sworn to do no wrong*
and does not take back his word.
    ⁶He does not give his money in hope of gain,*
    nor does he take a bribe against the innocent.
⁷Whoever does these things*
shall never be overthrown. Rx

Alternate tone

PFW 49

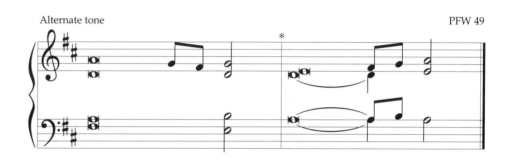

Sunday between July 24 and 30
Proper 12 | Psalm 138

Refrain

John Paradowski

Psalm tone

Your love en-dures for - ev - er; do not a-ban-don the works of your hands.

[1]I will give thanks to you, O Lord, with my whole heart;*
before the gods I will sing your praise.
  [2]**I will bow down toward your holy temple and praise your name,***
  because of your love and faithfulness;
[3]for you have glorified your name*
and your word above all things.
  [4]**When I called, you answered me;***
  you increased my strength within me. R
[5]All the kings of the earth will praise you, O Lord,*
when they have heard the words of your mouth.
  [6]**They will sing of the ways of the Lord,***
  that great is the glory of the Lord.
[7]Though the Lord be high, he cares for the lowly;*
he perceives the haughty from afar.
  [8]**Though I walk in the midst of trouble, you keep me safe;***
  you stretch forth your hand against the fury of my enemies;
  your right hand shall save me.
[9]The Lord will make good his purpose for me;*
O Lord, your love endures forever;
do not abandon the works of your hands. R

Alternate tone

Refrain

John Paradowski

We can nev - er ran - som our - selves or de -

We can nev - er ran - som our - selves or de -

liv - er to God the price of our life.

liv - er to God the price of our life.

[1]Hear this, all you peoples; hearken, all you who dwell ín the world,*
you of high degree and low, rich and póor together.

[2]My mouth shall spéak of wisdom,*
and my heart shall meditate on únderstanding. ℞

[3]I will incline my ear ío a proverb*
and set forth my riddle upón the harp.

[4]Why should I be afraid in évil days,*
when the wickedness of those at my héels surrounds me,

[5]the wickedness of those who put their trust ín their goods,*
and boast of théir great riches?

[6]We can never ranśom ourselves,*
or deliver to God the price óf our life;

[7]for the ransom of our life ís so great,*
that we should never have enóugh to pay it,

[8]in order to live forevér and ever,*
and never śee the grave. ℞

[9]For we see that the wise die also; like the dull and stupíd they perish*
and leave their wealth to those who come áfter them.

[10]Their graves shall be their homes forever,
their dwelling places from generation to géneration,*
though they call the lands after théir own names.

[11]Even though honored, they cannot líve forever;*
they are like the béasts that perish. ℞

Sunday between August 7 and 13

Proper 14 | Psalm 33:12-22

Refrain

John Paradowski

Let your lov - ing - kind - ness be up -

Let your lov - ing - kind - ness be up -

on us, as we have put our trust in you.

on us, as we have put our trust in you.

Psalm tone

[12]Happy is the nation whose God is the LORD!*
Happy the people he has chosen to be his own!
   [13]The LORD looks down from heaven,*
   and beholds all the people in the world.
[14]From where he sits enthroned he turns his gaze*
on all who dwell on the earth.
   [15]He fashions all the hearts of them*
   and understands all their works. ℟
[16]There is no king that can be saved by a mighty army;*
a strong man is not delivered by his great strength.
   [17]The horse is a vain hope for deliverance;*
   for all its strength it cannot save.
[18]Behold, the eye of the LORD is upon those who fear him,*
on those who wait upon his love,
   [19]to pluck their lives from death,*
   and to feed them in time of famine. ℟
[20]Our soul waits for the LORD;*
he is our help and our shield.
   [21]Indeed, our heart rejoices in him,*
   for in his holy name we put our trust.
[22]Let your lovingkindness, O LORD, be upon us,*
as we have put our trust in you. ℟

Alternate tone

Sunday between August 14 and 20

Proper 15 | Psalm 82

Refrain

John Paradowski

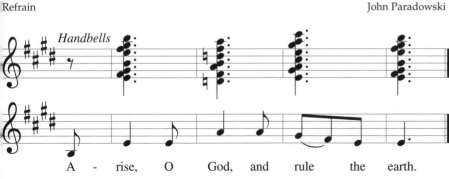

A - rise, O God, and rule the earth.

3-4 octaves
Handbells used: 14

[1]God takes his stand in the council of heaven;*
he gives judgment in the midst óf the gods:
  [2]"How long will you júdge unjustly,*
  and show favor ío the wicked?
[3]Save the weak ánd the orphan;*
defend the humble and needy;
  [4]rescue the weak ánd the poor;*
  deliver them from the power óf the wicked. ℞
[5]They do not know, neither do they understand; they go ábout in darkness;*
all the foundations of the éarth are shaken.
  [6]Now I say to you, 'Ýou are gods,*
  and all of you children of íhe Most High;
[7]nevertheless, you shall díe like mortals,*
and fall like ány prince.'"
  [8]Arise, O God, and rúle the earth,*
  for you shall take all nations fór your own. ℞

Sunday between August 21 and 27
Proper 16 | Psalm 103:1-8

Refrain

John Paradowski

The LORD crowns you with mer-cy and lov - ing - kind-ness.

The LORD crowns you with mer-cy and lov - ing - kind-ness.

Psalm tone

¹Bless the LORD, Ó my soul,*
and all that is within me, bless his hóly name.
  ²Bless the LORD, Ó my soul,*
  and forget not áll his benefits.
³He forgives áll your sins*
and heals all ýour infirmities;
  ⁴he redeems your life fróm the grave*
  and crowns you with mercy and lóvingkindness; R
⁵he satisfies you wíth good things,*
and your youth is renewed líke an eagle's.
  ⁶The LORD exécutes righteousness*
  and judgment for all who áre oppressed.
⁷He made his ways knówn to Moses*
and his works to the chíldren of Israel.
  ⁸The LORD is full of compasśion and mercy,*
  slow to anger and óf great kindness. R

Alternate tone

Sunday between Aug. 28 and Sept. 3
Proper 17 | Psalm 112

Refrain

John Paradowski

Psalm tone

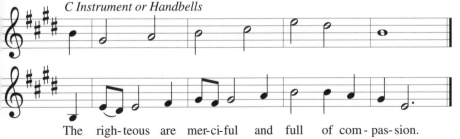

The righ-teous are mer-ci-ful and full of com-pas-sion.

[1]Hallelujah! Happy are they who fear the LORD*
and have great delight in his commandments!
   [2]Their descendants will be mighty in the land;*
   the generation of the upright will be blessed. ℟
[3]Wealth and riches will be in their house,*
and their righteousness will last forever.
   [4]Light shines in the darkness for the upright;*
   the righteous are merciful and full of compassion.
[5]It is good for them to be generous in lending*
and to manage their affairs with justice.
   [6]For they will never be shaken;*
   the righteous will be kept in everlasting remembrance. ℟
[7]They will not be afraid of any evil rumors;*
their heart is right; they put their trust in the LORD.
   [8]Their heart is established and will not shrink,*
   until they see their desire upon their enemies.
[9]They have given freely to the poor,*
and their righteousness stands fast forever;
they will hold up their head with honor.
   [10]The wicked will see it and be angry;*
   they will gnash their teeth and pine away;*
   the desires of the wicked will perish. ℟

Alternate accompaniment

Alternate tone

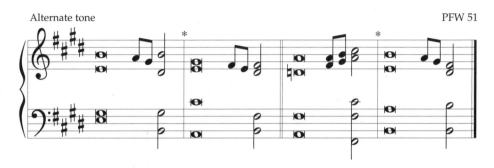

Sunday between September 4 and 10
Proper 18 | Psalm 1

Refrain

Dorothy Christopherson

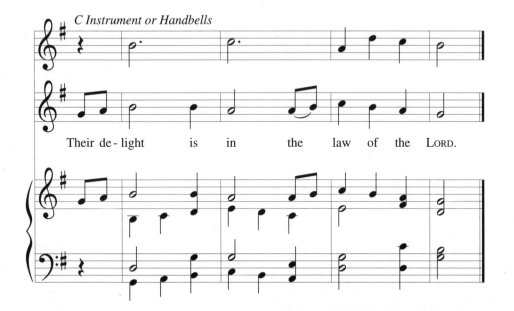

Their de-light is in the law of the LORD.

Psalm tone

[1]Happy are they who have not walked in the counsel óf the wicked,*
nor lingered in the way of sinners, nor sat in the seats óf the scornful!
    [2]Their delight is in the law óf the LORD,*
    and they meditate on his law day and night. ℟
[3]They are like trees planted by streams of water,
bearing fruit in due season, with leaves that do not wither;*
everything they do shall prosper.
    [4]It is not so with the wicked;*
    they are like chaff which the wind blows away.
[5]Therefore the wicked shall not stand upright when judgment comes,*
nor the sinner in the council óf the righteous.
    [6]For the LORD knows the way óf the righteous,*
    but the way of the wickéd is doomed. ℟

Alternate tone

Sunday between September 11 and 17

Proper 19 | Psalm 51:1-11

Psalm tone

Refrain

Dorothy Christopherson

Have mer-cy on me, O God, ac-

cord-ing to your lov-ing kind-ness.

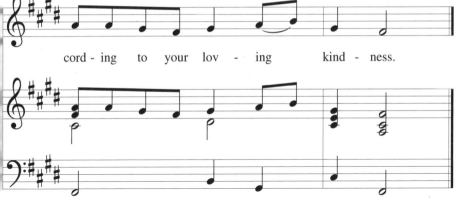

[1]Have mercy on me, O God, according to your lovingkindness;*
in your great compassion blot out my offenses.
   [2]**Wash me through and through from my wickedness,***
   and cleanse me from my sin.
[3]For I know my transgressions,*
and my sin is ever before me.
   [4]**Against you only have I sinned***
   and done what is evil in your sight. ℟
[5]And so you are justified when you speak*
and upright in your judgment.
   [6]**Indeed, I have been wicked from my birth,***
   a sinner from my mother's womb.
[7]For behold, you look for truth deep within me,*
and will make me understand wisdom secretly.
   [8]**Purge me from my sin, and I shall be pure;***
   wash me, and I shall be clean indeed. ℟
[9]Make me hear of joy and gladness,*
that the body you have broken may rejoice.
   [10]**Hide your face from my sins,***
   and blot out all my iniquities.
[11]Create in me a clean heart, O God,*
and renew a right spirit within me. ℟

Alternate tone

PFW 52

Sunday between September 18 and 24
Proper 20 | Psalm 113

Refrain

Dorothy Christopherson

The LORD lifts up the poor from the ash - es.

[1]Hallelujah! Give praise, you servants óf the LORD;*
praise the name óf the LORD.
   [2]Let the name of the LÓRD be blessed,*
   from this time forth forévermore.
[3]From the rising of the sun to its góing down*
let the name of the LÓRD be praised.
   [4]The LORD is high abóve all nations,*
   and his glory above the heavens. R̩
[5]Who is like the LORD our God, who sits enthroned on high,*
but stoops to behold the heavens ánd the earth?
   [6]He takes up the weak out óf the dust*
   and lifts up the poor fróm the ashes.
[7]He sets them with the princes,*
with the princes óf his people.
   [8]He makes the woman of a childless house*
   to be a joyful mothér of children. R̩

Alternate tone

Sunday between Sept. 25 and Oct. 1

Proper 21 | Psalm 146

Refrain

Dorothy Christopherson

The LORD gives jus - tice, the

LORD gives jus - tice to those who are op - pressed.

2 octaves
Handbells used: 7

Psalm tone

¹Hallelujah! Praise the LORD, Ó my soul!*
I will praise the LORD as long as I live;
I will sing praises to my God while I h́ave my being.
  ²Put not your trust in rulers, nor in any ćhild of earth,*
  for there is no h́elp in them. ℞
³When they breathe their last, they ret́urn to earth,*
and in that day t́heir thoughts perish.
  ⁴Happy are they who have the God of Jacob f́or their help,*
  whose hope is in the ĹORD their God;
⁵who made heaven and earth, the seas, and all that ́is in them;*
who keeps his proḿise forever;
  ⁶who gives justice to those who áre oppressed,*
  and food to t́hose who hunger. ℞
⁷The LORD sets the prisoners free; the LORD opens the eyes óf the blind;*
the LORD lifts up those who áre bowed down;
  ⁸the LORD loves the righteous; the LORD cares f́or the stranger;*
  he sustains the orphan and widow,
  but frustrates the way óf the wicked.
⁹The LORD shall f́eign forever,*
your God, O Zion, throughout all generations. H́allelujah! ℞

Alternate tone

PFW 52

Sunday between October 2 and 8
Proper 22 | Psalm 37:1-10

Refrain

Dorothy Christopherson

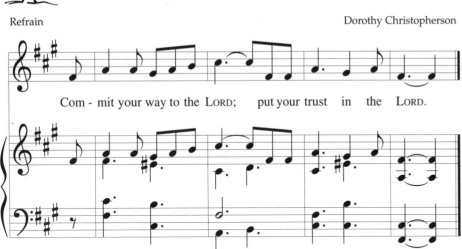

Com - mit your way to the LORD; put your trust in the LORD.

[1]Do not fret yourself because of évildoers;*
do not be jealous of those who do wrong.
   [2]For they shall soon wither like the grass,*
   and like the green grass fade away.
[3]Put your trust in the LORD ánd do good;*
dwell in the land and feed ón its riches.
   [4]Take delight in the LORD,*
   and he shall give you your heart's desire. ℟
[5]Commit your way to the LORD and put your trust in him,*
and he will bring it to pass.
   [6]He will make your righteousness as clear ás the light*
   and your just dealing ás the noonday.
[7]Be still before the LORD*
and wait patiently for him.
   [8]Do not fret yourself over the óne who prospers,*
   the one who succeeds in évil schemes.
[9]Refrain from anger, leave rage alone;*
do not fret yourself; it leads only to evil.
   [10]For evildoers shall be cut off,*
   but those who wait upon the LORD shall possess the land. ℟

Sunday between October 9 and 15
Proper 23 | Psalm 111

Refrain

Dorothy Christopherson

I will give thanks, I will give thanks to the

Lord with my whole heart.

2 octaves
Handbells used: 6

Psalm tone

[1]Hallelujah! I will give thanks to the LORD with my whole heart,*
in the assembly of the upright, in the congregation.
    [2]Great are the deeds óf the LORD!*
    They are studied by all who delíght in them. R̂
[3]His work is full of majestý and splendor,*
and his righteousness endúres forever.
    [4]He makes his marvelous works to bé remembered;*
    the LORD is gracious and full óf compassion.
[5]He gives food to thóse who fear him;*
he is ever mindful óf his covenant.
    [6]He has shown his people the power óf his works*
    in giving them the lands óf the nations. R̂
[7]The works of his hands are faithfulnéss and justice;*
all his commandménts are sure.
    [8]They stand fast forevér and ever,*
    because they are done in trúth and equity.
[9]He sent redemption to his people; he commanded his covénant forever;*
holy and awesome ís his name.
    [10]The fear of the LORD is the beginníng of wisdom;*
    those who act accordingly have a good understanding.
    His praise endúres forever. R̂

Alternate tone

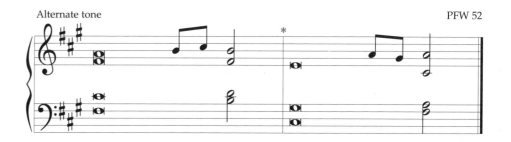

Sunday between October 16 and 22
Proper 24 | Psalm 121

Refrain

Dorothy Christopherson

My help comes from the LORD,

My help comes from the LORD, the

mak - er of heav - en and earth.

mak - er of heav - en and earth.

[1]I lift up my eyes to the hills;*
from where is my help to come?
   [2]My help comes from the LORD,*
   the maker of heaven and earth.
[3]He will not let your foot be moved*
and he who watches over you will not fall asleep.
   [4]Behold, he who keeps watch over Israel*
   shall neither slumber nor sleep; ℟
[5]the LORD himself watches over you;*
the LORD is your shade at your right hand,
   [6]so that the sun shall not strike you by day,*
   nor the moon by night.
[7]The LORD shall preserve you from all evil;*
it is he who shall keep you safe.
   [8]The LORD shall watch over your going out and your coming in,*
   from this time forth forevermore. ℟

Alternate tone

PFW 52

Sunday between October 23 and 29

Proper 25 | Psalm 84:1-6

Refrain

David Cherwien

Hap - py are the peo - ple whose strength is in you.

Psalm tone

[1]How dear to me is your dwelling, O LORD of hosts!*
My soul has a desire and longing for the courts of the LORD;
my heart and my flesh rejoice in the líving God.

 [2]The sparrow has found her a house
 and the swallow a nest where she may láy her young,*
 by the side of your altars, O LORD of hosts, my King ánd my God. ℟
[3]Happy are they who dwell ín your house!*
They will always be práising you.
 [4]Happy are the people whose strength ís in you,*
 whose hearts are set on the pílgrims' way.
[5]Those who go through the desolate valley will find it a pláce of springs,*
for the early rains have covered it with póols of water.
 [6]They will climb from héight to height,*
 and the God of gods will reveal hímself in Zion. ℟

Alternate tone

Sunday between Oct. 30 and Nov. 5
Proper 26 | Psalm 32:1-8

Refrain

David Cherwien

Psalm tone

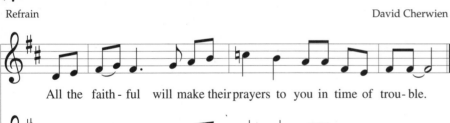

All the faith-ful will make their prayers to you in time of trou-ble.

[1]Happy are they whose transgressions áre forgiven,*
and whose sin is put away!

  [2]Happy are they to whom the LORD impútes no guilt,*
  and in whose spirit there ís no guile!

[3]While I held my tongue, my bones withéred away,*
because of my groaning áll day long.

  [4]For your hand was heavy upon me day and night;*
  my moisture was dried up as in the heat of summer. R

[5]Then I acknowledged my sín to you,*
and did not conceal my guilt.

  [6]I said, "I will confess my transgressions to the LORD."*
  Then you forgave me the guilt óf my sin.

[7]Therefore all the faithful will make their prayers to you in time of trou
when the great waters overflow, they shall not reach them.

  [8]You are my hiding place; you preserve me from trouble;
  you surround me with shouts óf deliverance. R

Alternate tone

Sunday between November 6 and 12

Proper 27 | Psalm 17:1-9

Refrain

David Cherwien

Slowly

Keep me as the ap-ple of your eye;

hide me un-der the shad-ow of your wings.

Psalm tone

[1]Hear my plea of innocence, O Lord; give heed to my cry;*
listen to my prayer, which does not come from lying lips.
> [2]**Let my vindication come forth from your presence;***
> **let your eyes be fixed on justice.**
[3]Weigh my heart, summon me by night,*
melt me down; you will find no impurity in me.
> [4]**I give no offense with my mouth as others do;***
> **I have heeded the words of your lips. ℟**
[5]My footsteps hold fast to the ways of your law;*
in your paths my feet shall not stumble.
> [6]**I call upon you, O God, for you will answer me;***
> **incline your ear to me and hear my words.**
[7]Show me your marvelous lovingkindness,*
O Savior of those who take refuge at your right hand
from those who rise up against them.
> [8]**Keep me as the apple of your eye;***
> **hide me under the shadow of your wings,**
[9]from the wicked who assault me,*
from my deadly enemies who surround me. ℟

Alternate tone

Sunday between November 13 and 19
Proper 28 | Psalm 98

Psalm tone

Refrain

David Cherwien

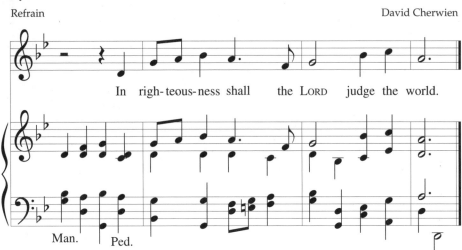

In righ-teous-ness shall the LORD judge the world.

Man. Ped.

[1]Sing to the LORD a new song,*
for he has done marvelous things.
   [2]**With his right hand and his holy arm***
   has he won for himself the victory.
[3]The LORD has made known his victory;*
his righteousness has he openly shown in the sight of the nations.
   [4]**He remembers his mercy and faithfulness to the house of Israel,***
   and all the ends of the earth have seen the victory of our God. R
[5]Shout with joy to the LORD, all you lands;*
lift up your voice, rejoice, and sing.
   [6]**Sing to the LORD with the harp,***
   with the harp and the voice of song.
[7]With trumpets and the sound of the horn*
shout with joy before the king, the LORD.
   [8]**Let the sea make a noise and all that is in it,***
   the lands and those who dwell therein.
[9]Let the rivers clap their hands,*
and let the hills ring out with joy before the LORD,
when he comes to judge the earth.
   [10]**In righteousness shall he judge the world***
   and the peoples with equity. R

Alternate tone

Christis the King
Sunday between Nov. 20 and 26
Last Sunday after Pentecost
Proper 29 | Psalm 46

David Cherwien

Refrain

I will be ex-alt-ed a-mong the na-tions.

Man.   Ped.

[1]God is our refuge and strength,*
a very present help in trouble.
   [2]**Therefore we will not fear, though the éarth be moved,***
   and though the mountains be toppled into the depths óf the sea;
[3]though its waters ŕage and foam,*
and though the mountains tremble át its tumult.
   [4]**The LORD of hósts is with us;***
   the God of Jacob ís our stronghold. R
[5]There is a river whose streams make glad the citý of God,*
the holy habitation of t́he Most High.
   [6]**God is in the midst of her; she shall not be óverthrown;***
   God shall help her at the b́reak of day.
[7]The nations make much ado, and the kingd́oms are shaken;*
God has spoken, and the earth shall ḿelt away.
   [8]**The LORD of hósts is with us;***
   the God of Jacob ís our stronghold. R
[9]Come now and look upon the works óf the LORD,*
what awesome things he has d́one on earth.
   [10]**It is he who makes war to cease in áll the world;***
   he breaks the bow, and shatters the spear, and burns the śhields with fire.
[11]"Be still, then, and know that Í am God;*
I will be exalted among the nations; I will be exalted ín the earth."
   [12]**The LORD of hósts is with us;***
   the God of Jacob ís our stronghold. R

St. Andrew, Apostle
November 30 | Psalm 19:1-6

Refrain

Thomas Pavlechko

3 octaves
Handbells used: 12

[1]The heavens declare the glory of God,*
and the firmament shows his handiwork.
   [2]**One day tells its tale to another,***
   and one night imparts knowledge to another.
[3]Although they have no words or language,*
and their voices are not heard,
   [4]**their sound has gone out into all lands,***
   and their message to the ends of the world. R
[5]In the deep has he set a pavilion for the sun;*
it comes forth like a bridegroom out of his chamber;
it rejoices like a champion to run its course.
   [6]**It goes forth from the uttermost edge of the heavens**
   and runs about to the end of it again;*
   nothing is hidden from its burning heat. R

Alternate tone

St. Thomas, Apostle
December 21 | Psalm 136:1-4, 23-26

Refrain

Thomas Pavlechko

Psalm tone

[Music: Refrain with "God's mer-cy en-dures for-ev-er." repeated]

¹Give thanks to the Lord, for he is good,*
for his mercy endures forever.
    ²Give thanks to the God of gods,*
    for his mercy endures forever.
³Give thanks to the Lord of lords,*
for his mercy endures forever;
    ⁴who only does great wonders,*
    for his mercy endures forever; R
²³who remembered us in our low estate,*
for his mercy endures forever;
    ²⁴and delivered us from our enemies,*
    for his mercy endures forever;
²⁵who gives food to all creatures,*
for his mercy endures forever.
    ²⁶Give thanks to the God of heaven,*
    for his mercy endures forever. R

Alternate tone

St. Stephen, Deacon and Martyr
December 26 | Psalm 17:1-9, 16

Refrain

Thomas Pavlechko

Handbells

Finger Cymbals

Descant

I call up-on you, O God, you an-swer me.

I call up-on you, O God, for you will an-swer me.

2 octaves
Handbells used: 10

[1]Hear my plea of innocence, O Lord; give heed to my cry;*
listen to my prayer, which does not come from lying lips.
 [2]**Let my vindication come forth from your presence;***
 let your eyes be fixed on justice. ℟
[3]Weigh my heart, summon me by night,*
melt me down; you will find no impurity in me.
 [4]**I give no offense with my mouth as others do;***
 I have heeded the words of your lips.
[5]My footsteps hold fast to the ways of your law;*
in your paths my feet shall not stumble.
 [6]**I call upon you, O God, for you will answer me;***
 incline your ear to me and hear my words. ℟
[7]Show me your marvelous lovingkindness,*
O Savior of those who take refuge at your right hand
from those who rise up against them.
 [8]**Keep me as the apple of your eye;***
 hide me under the shadow of your wings,
[9]from the wicked who assault me,*
from my deadly enemies who surround me.
 [16]**But at my vindication I shall see your face;***
 when I awake, I shall be satisfied, beholding your likeness. ℟

St. John, Apostle and Evangelist
December 27 | Psalm 116:10-17

Refrain

Thomas Pavlechko

Psalm tone

Pre - cious in your sight, O LORD, is the

Pre - cious in your sight, O LORD, is the

death of your ser - vants.

death of your ser - vants.

[10]How shall I repay the LORD*
for all the good things he has done for me?
    [11]I will lift up the cup óf salvation*
    and call upon the name óf the LORD.
[12]I will fulfill my vows to the LORD*
in the presence of áll his people.
    [13]Precious in the sight óf the LORD*
    is the death óf his servants. R︎
[14]O LORD, I ám your servant;*
I am your servant and the child of your handmaid;
you have freed me from my bonds.
    [15]I will offer you the sacrifice óf thanksgiving*
    and call upon the name óf the LORD.
[16]I will fulfill my vows to the LORD*
in the presence of áll his people,
    [17]in the courts of the LORD's house,*
    in the midst of you, O Jerusalem. Hallelujah! R︎

Alternate tone

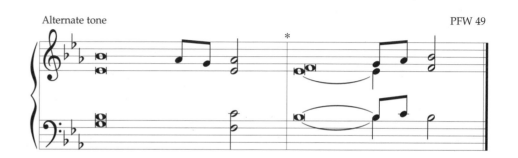

The Holy Innocents, Martyrs

December 28 | Psalm 124

Refrain

Thomas Pavlechko

Flute

Handbells

Descant

We have es - caped like a

We have es - caped like a

bird from the snare of the fowl - er.

bird from the snare of the fowl - er.

2 octaves
Handbells used: 12

¹If the LORD had not been ón our side,*
let Israél now say;

   ²if the LORD had not been ón our side,*
   when enemies rose úp against us,

³then would they have swallowed us úp alive*
in their fierce ánger toward us;

   ⁴then would the waters have óverwhelmed us*
   and the torrent gone óver us; ℟

⁵then would the ŕaging waters*
have gone right óver us.

   ⁶Blessed b́e the LORD!*
   He has not given us over to be a prey f́or their teeth.

⁷We have escaped like a bird from the snare óf the fowler;*
the snare is broken, and we h́ave escaped.

   ⁸Our help is in the name óf the LORD,*
   the maker of heavén and earth. ℟

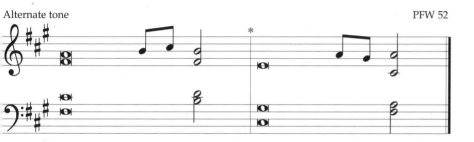

The Name of Jesus

January 1 | Psalm 8

Refrain

Michael Hassell

(♩=76-80)

How ex - al - ted is your name in all the world, all the world,

Am   F   C/G   E   Am

how ex - al - ted is your name in all the world!

Em   F   C/G   G⁷   C

Psalm tone

¹O Lᴏʀᴅ our Lord,*
how exalted is your name in áll the world!
　²Out of the mouths of inf́ants and children*
　your majesty is praised ab́ove the heavens. Ŗ
³You have set up a stronghold against your ádversaries,*
to quell the enemy and t́he avenger.
　⁴When I consider your heavens, the work óf your fingers,*
　the moon and the stars you have set ín their courses,
⁵what is man that you should be mindf́ul of him,*
the son of man that you should śeek him out?
　⁶You have made him but little lower t́han the angels;*
　you adorn him with glor̃y and honor; Ŗ
⁷you give him mastery over the works óf your hands;*
you put all things und́er his feet:
　⁸all śheep and oxen,*
　even the wild beasts óf the field,
⁹the birds of the air, the fish óf the sea,*
and whatsoever walks in the paths óf the sea.
　¹⁰O Lᴏʀᴅ our Lord,*
　how exalted is your name in áll the world! Ŗ

Alternate tone

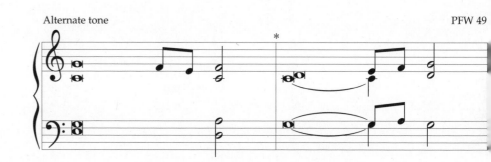

The Confession of St. Peter

January 18 | Psalm 18:1-7, 17-20

Refrain

Thomas Pavlechko

My God, my rock, you are wor - thy of praise.

My God, my rock, you are wor - thy of praise.

2 octaves
Handbells used: 11

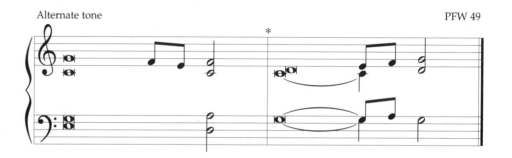

¹I love you, O LORD my strength,*
O LORD my stronghold, my crag, ánd my haven.
  ²My God, my rock in whom I put my trust,*
  my shield, the horn of my salvation, and my refuge: You are worthý of praise. ℞
³I will call upón the LORD,*
and so shall I be saved from my enemies.
  ⁴The breakers of death rolled óver me,*
  and the torrents of oblivion made me afraid.
⁵The cords of hell entangled me,*
and the snares of death were set for me.
  ⁶I called upon the LORD in my distress*
  and cried out to my God for help. ℞
⁷He heard my voice from his heavénly dwelling;*
my cry of anguish came to his ears.
  ¹⁷He reached down from on high and grasped me;*
  he drew me out óf great waters.
¹⁸He delivered me from my strong enemies and from those who hated me,*
for they were too mighty for me.
  ¹⁹They confronted me in the day of my disaster;*
  but the LORD was my support.
²⁰He brought me out into an ópen place;*
he rescued me because he delightéd in me. ℞

Alternate tone

PFW 49

The Conversion of St. Paul

January 25 | Psalm 67

Refrain

Thomas Pavlechko

Handbells

Descant

Let all the peo-ples praise you, O God.

Let all the peo-ples praise you, O God.

optional introduction

[1]May God be merciful to ús and bless us,*
show us the light of his countenance, and ćome to us.
   [2]Let your ways be known úpon earth,*
   your saving health amóng all nations.
[3]Let the peoples praise ýou, O God;*
let all the péoples praise you.
   [4]Let the nations be glad and śing for joy,*
   for you judge the peoples with equity
   and guide all the nations úpon earth. ℞
[5]Let the peoples praise ýou, O God;*
let all the péoples praise you.
   [6]The earth has brought fórth her increase;*
   may God, our own God, give ús his blessing.
[7]May God give ús his blessing,*
and may all the ends of the earth stand in áwe of him. ℞

2 octaves
Handbells used: 11

Alternate tone

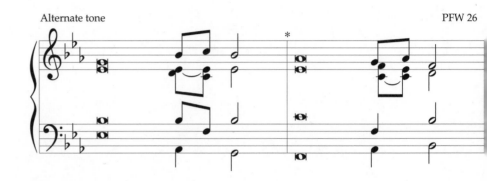

The Presentation of Our Lord

February 2 | Psalm 84

LBW 1

Thomas Pavlechko
(after Johannes Brahms)

Refrain

Handbells

Psalm tone

Countermelody (may also be sung an octave lower)

How dear to me, how dear is your dwell-ing, O LORD.

How dear to me is your dwell - ing, O LORD.

[1]How dear to me is your dwelling, O LORD of hosts!*
My soul has a desire and longing for the courts of the LORD;
my heart and my flesh rejoice in the living God.
   **[2]The sparrow has found her a house
   and the swallow a nest where she may lay her young,***
   by the side of your altars, O LORD of hosts, my King and my God.
[3]Happy are they who dwell in your house!*
They will always be praising you.
   [4]Happy are the people whose strength is in you,*
   whose hearts are set on the pilgrims' way. R
[5]Those who go through the desolate valley will find it a place of springs,*
for the early rains have covered it with pools of water.
   [6]They will climb from height to height,*
   and the God of gods will reveal himself in Zion.
[7]LORD God of hosts, hear my prayer;*
hearken, O God of Jacob.
   [8]Behold our defender, O God;*
   and look upon the face of your anointed. R
[9]For one day in your courts is better than a thousand in my own room,*
and to stand at the threshold of the house of my God
than to dwell in the tents of the wicked.
   [10]For the LORD God is both sun and shield;*
   he will give grace and glory;
[11]no good thing will the LORD withhold*
from those who walk with integrity.
   [12]O LORD of hosts,*
   happy are they who put their trust in you! R

2 octaves
Handbells used: 10

Alternate tone

PFW 22

St. Matthias, Apostle
February 24 | Psalm 56

Thomas Pavlechko

Refrain

bound by the vow   I   made,   O   God.

I am bound   by the vow   I   made to you, O God.

[1]Have mercy on me, O God, for my enemies are hounding me;*
all day long they assault and oppress me.
> [2]**They hound me all the day long;***
> **truly there are many who fight against me, O Most High.**

[3]Whenever I am afraid,*
I will put my trust in you.
> [4]**In God, whose word I praise, in God I trust and will not be afraid,***
> **for what can flesh do to me? ℟**

[5]All day long they damage my cause;*
their only thought is to do me evil.
> [6]**They band together; they lie in wait;***
> **they spy upon my footsteps; because they seek my life.**

[7]Shall they escape despite their wickedness?*
O God, in your anger, cast down the peoples.
> [8]**You have noted my lamentation; put my tears into your bottle;***
> **are they not recorded in your book? ℟**

[9]Whenever I call upon you, my enemies will be put to flight;*
this I know, for God is on my side.
> [10]**In God the Lord, whose word I praise, in God I trust and will not be afraid,***
> **for what can mortals do to me?**

[11]I am bound by the vow I made to you, O God;*
I will present to you thank-offerings;
> [12]**for you have rescued my soul from death and my feet from stumbling,***
> **that I may walk before God in the light of the living. ℟**

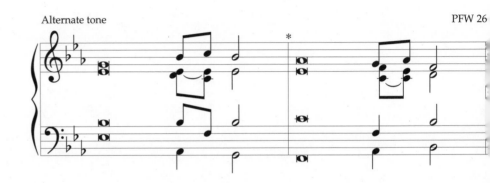

The Annunciation of Our Lord
March 25 | Psalm 40:5-11

Refrain

John Folkening

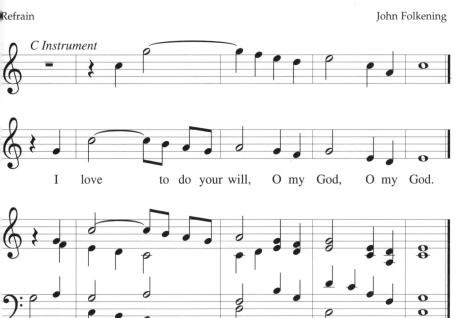

I love to do your will, O my God, O my God.

Psalm tone

[5]Great things are they that you have done, O LORD my God!
How great your wonders and your plans for us!*
There is none who can be compared with you.
   [6]Oh, that I could make them known and tell them!*
   But they are more than I can count.
[7]In sacrifice and offering you take no pleasure;*
you have given me ears to hear you;
   [8]burnt-offering and sin-offering you have not required,*
   and so I said, "Behold, I come. R̲
[9]In the roll of the book it is written concerning me:*
'I love to do your will, O my God; your law is deep in my heart.'"
   [10]I proclaimed righteousness in the great congregation;*
   behold, I did not restrain my lips; and that, O LORD, you know.
[11]Your righteousness have I not hidden in my heart;
I have spoken of your faithfulness and your deliverance;*
I have not concealed your love and faithfulness
from the great congregation. R̲

Alternate tone

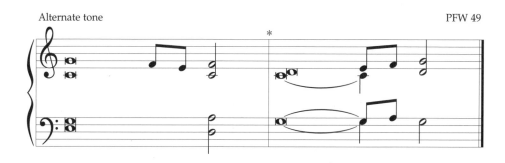

Psalm 45 (Psalter for Worship, Cycle C, p.110)

St. Mark, Evangelist

April 25 | Psalm 57

Refrain

Ronald Turner

I will con-fess you a-mong the peo-ples, O Lord.

Psalm tone

[1]Be merciful to me, O God, be merciful, for I have taken refúge in you;*
in the shadow of your wings will I take refuge
until this time of trouble has gone by.
   [2]I will call upon the Móst High God,*
   the God who maintáins my cause. ℟
[3]He will send from heaven and save me;
he will confound those who trample upon me;*
God will send forth his love ánd his faithfulness.
   [4]I lie in the midst of lions that devóur the people;*
   their teeth are spears and arrows, their tongue á sharp sword.
[5]They have laid a net for my feet, and I ám bowed low;*
they have dug a pit before me, but have fallen into ít themselves.
   [6]Exalt yourself above the heavéns, O God,*
   and your glory over áll the earth. ℟
[7]My heart is firmly fixed, O God, my héart is fixed;*
I will sing ánd make melody.
   [8]Wake up, my spirit; awake, lúte and harp;*
   I myself will wakén the dawn.
[9]I will confess you among the peóples, O Lord;*
I will sing praise to you amóng the nations.
   [10]For your lovingkindness is greater thán the heavens,*
   and your faithfulness reaches ío the clouds.
[11]Exalt yourself above the heavéns, O God,*
and your glory over áll the earth. ℟

Alternate tone

St. Philip and St. James, Apostles

May 1 | Psalm 44:1-3, 20-26

Refrain

Ronald Turner

Save us, save us for the sake of your stead-fast love.

Psalm tone

[1]We have heard with our ears, O God, our forefathers have told us,*
the deeds you did in their days, in the days of old.
  [2]How with your hand you drove the peoples out
  and planted our forefathers in the land;*
  how you destroyed nations and made your people flourish. R
[3]For they did not take the land by their sword,
nor did their arm win the victory for them;*
but your right hand, your arm, and the light of your countenance,
because you favored them.
  [20]If we have forgotten the name of our God,*
  or stretched out our hands to some strange god,
[21]will not God find it out?*
For he knows the secrets of the heart.
  [22]Indeed, for your sake we are killed all the day long;*
  we are accounted as sheep for the slaughter. R
[23]Awake, O Lord! Why are you sleeping?*
Arise! Do not reject us forever.
  [24]Why have you hidden your face*
  and forgotten our affliction and oppression?
[25]We sink down into the dust;*
our body cleaves to the ground.
  [26]Rise up, and help us,*
  and save us, for the sake of your steadfast love. R

Alternate tone

The Visitation
May 31 | Psalm 113

Refrain

Carolyn Jennings

Let the name of the LORD be

blessed from this time forth for - ev - er - more.

¹Hallelujah! Give praise, you servants óf the LORD;*
praise the name óf the LORD.
   ²Let the name of the LÓRD be blessed,*
   from this time forth forévermore.
³From the rising of the sun to its góing down*
let the name of the LÓRD be praised.
   ⁴The LORD is high abóve all nations,*
   and his glory abóve the heavens. R
⁵Who is like the LORD our God, who sits ent́hroned on high,*
but stoops to behold the heavens ánd the earth?
   ⁶He takes up the weak out óf the dust*
   and lifts up the poor f́rom the ashes.
⁷He sets them with́ the princes,*
with the princes óf his people.
   ⁸He makes the woman of a chíldless house*
   to be a joyful mothér of children. R

St. Barnabas, Apostle
June 11 | Psalm 112

Refrain

Ronald Turner

Psalm tone

Hap-py are they who fear the LORD, who fear the LORD.

¹Hallelujah!
Happy are they who fear the LORD*
and have great delight in his commandments!
   ²Their descendants will be mighty in the land;*
   the generation of the upright will be blessed.
³Wealth and riches will be in their house,*
and their righteousness will last forever.
   ⁴Light shines in the darkness for the upright;*
   the righteous are merciful and full of compassion. ℞
⁵It is good for them to be generous in their lending*
and to manage their affairs with justice.
   ⁶For they will never be shaken,*
   the righteous will be kept in everlasting remembrance. ℞
⁷They will not be afraid of any evil rumors;*
their heart is right; they put their trust in the LORD.
   ⁸Their heart is established and will not shrink,*
   until they see their desire upon their enemies.
⁹They have given freely to the poor,*
and their righteousness stands fast forever;
they will hold up their head with honor.
   ¹⁰The wicked will see it and be angry;*
   they will gnash their teeth and pine away;*
   the desires of the wicked will perish. ℞

Alternate tone

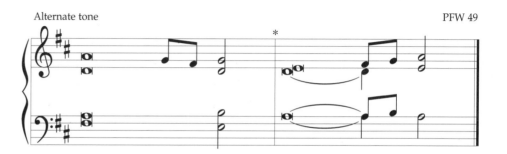

The Nativity of St. John the Baptist
June 24 | Psalm 141

Refrain

Ronald Turner

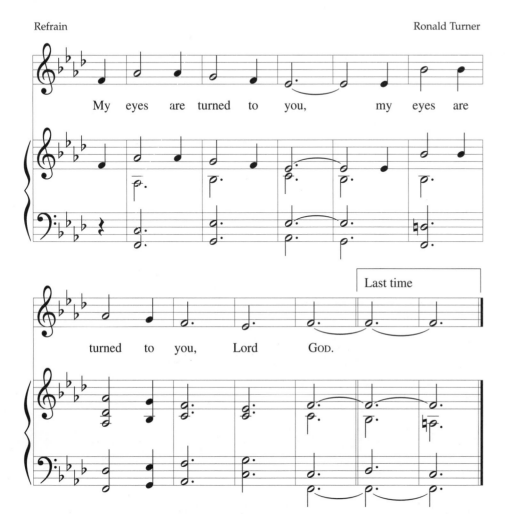

My eyes are turned to you, my eyes are

Last time

turned to you, Lord GOD.

Psalm tone

[1] O Lord, I call to you; come to me quickly;*
hear my voice when I cry to you.
  [2] Let my prayer be set forth in your sight as incense,*
  the lifting up of my hands as the evening sacrifice.
[3] Set a watch before my mouth, O Lord, and guard the door of my lips;*
let not my heart incline to any evil thing.
  [4] Let me not be occupied in wickedness with evildoers,*
  nor eat of their choice foods. R
[5] Let the righteous smite me in friendly rebuke;
let not the oil of the unrighteous anoint my head;*
for my prayer is continually against their wicked deeds.
  [6] Let their rulers be overthrown in stony places,*
  that they may know my words are true.
[7] As when a plowman turns over the earth in furrows,*
let their bones be scattered at the mouth of the grave.
  [8] But my eyes are turned to you, Lord GOD;*
  in you I take refuge; do not strip me of my life. R
[9] Protect me from the snare which they have laid for me*
and from the traps of the evildoers.
  [10] Let the wicked fall into their own nets,*
  while I myself escape. R

Alternate tone

St. Peter and St. Paul, Apostles

June 29 | Psalm 87:1-2, 4-6

Refrain

Anne Krentz Organ

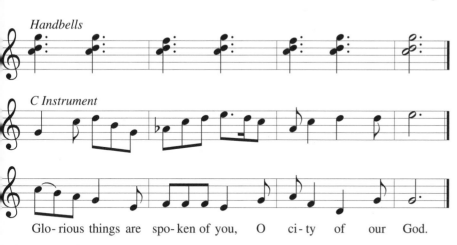

Glo- rious things are spo- ken of you, O ci- ty of our God.

[1]On the holy mountain stands the city he has founded;*
the LORD loves the gates of Zion more than all the dwellings of Jacob.
    [2]Glorious things are spoken of you,*
    O city of our God. ℞
[4]Of Zion it shall be said, "Everyone was born in her,*
and the Most High himself shall sustain her."
    [5]The LORD will record as he enrolls the peoples,*
    "These also were born there."
[6]The singers and the dancers will say,*
"All my fresh springs are in you." **℞**

St. Mary Magdalene

July 22 | Psalm 73:23-29

Carolyn Jennings

Refrain

C Instrument

Descant

I will speak of all your works in the gates of Zi- on.

I will speak of all your works in the gates of the cit- y of Zi- on.

²³Yet I am always with you;*
you hold me by my right hand.
  ²⁴You will guide me by your counsel,*
  and afterwards receive me with glory.
²⁵Whom have I in heaven but you?*
And having you, I desire nothing upon earth.
  ²⁶Though my flesh and my heart should waste away,*
  God is the strength of my heart and my portion forever. R
²⁷Truly, those who forsake you will perish;*
you destroy all who are unfaithful.
  ²⁸But it is good for me to be near God;*
  I have made the Lord God my refuge.
²⁹I will speak of all your works*
in the gates of the city of Zion. R

Alternate tone

St. James the Elder, Apostle

July 25 | Psalm 7:1-11

Refrain

Ronald Turner

Descant

God is my shield, my shield and de-fense.

God is my shield, my shield and de-fense.

Psalm tone

[1]O Lord my God, I take refúge in you;*
save and deliver me from all who pursue me;
   [2]**lest like a lion they tear me in pieces***
   and snatch me away with none to delíver me. ℞
[3]O Lord my God, if I have done these things:*
if there is any wickedness ín my hands,
   [4]**if I have repaid my fríend with evil,***
   or plundered him who without cause ís my enemy,
[5]then let my enemy pursue and óvertake me,*
trample my life into the ground, and lay my honor ín the dust.
   [6]**Stand up, O Lord, ín your wrath;***
   rise up against the fury óf my enemies. ℞
[7]Awake, O my God, decree justice;*
let the assembly of the peoples gather round you.
   [8]**Be seated on your lofty throne, Ó Most High;***
   O Lord, judge the nations.
[9]Give judgment for me according to my righteousńess, O Lord,*
and according to my innocence, Ó Most High.
   [10]**Let the malice of the wicked come to an end, but establísh the righteous;***
   for you test the mind and heart, O ríghteous God.
[11]God is my shield ánd defense;*
he is the savior of the trúe in heart. ℞

Alternate tone

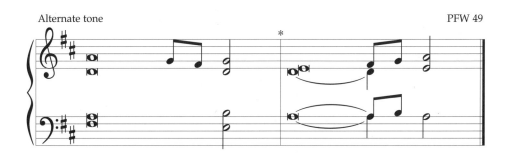

Mary, Mother of Our Lord

August 15 | Psalm 45:11-16

Refrain

Carolyn Jennings

[11]"Hear, O daughter; consider and lîsten closely;*
forget your people and your fâther's house.
   [12]The king will have pleasure în your beauty;*
   he is your master; therefore dô him honor.
[13]The people of Tyre are here wîth a gift;*
the rich among the people sêek your favor."
   [14]All glorious is the princess âs she enters;*
   her gown is clôth-of-gold. Rx
[15]In embroidered apparel she is brought îo the king;*
after her the bridesmaids follow în procession.
   [16]With joy and gladness thêy are brought,*
   and enter into the palace ôf the king. Rx

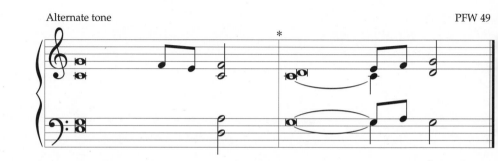

St. Bartholomew, Apostle

August 24 | Psalm 12

Refrain

Anne Krentz Organ

C Instrument

The words of the LORD are pure.

Psalm tone

[1]Help me, LORD, for there is no godly one left;*
the faithful have vanished from among us.
    [2]Everyone speaks falsely with his neighbor;*
    with a smooth tongue they speak from a double heart.
[3]Oh, that the LORD would cut off all smooth tongues,*
and close the lips that utter proud boasts!
    [4]Those who say, "With our tongue will we prevail;*
    our lips are our own; who is lord over us?" R
[5]"Because the needy are oppressed, and the poor cry out in misery,*
I will rise up," says the LORD, "and give them the help they long for."
    [6]The words of the LORD are pure words,*
    like silver refined from ore and purified seven times in the fire.
[7]O LORD, watch over us*
and save us from this generation forever.
    [8]The wicked prowl on every side,*
    and that which is worthless is highly prized by everyone. R

Alternate tone

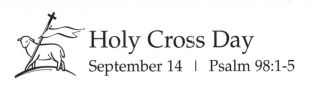

Holy Cross Day
September 14 | Psalm 98:1-5

Refrain

Anne Krentz Organ

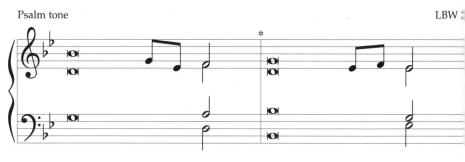

Bb Trumpet

Descant

The LORD, the LORD has done mar - vel - ous things.

The LORD has done mar - vel - ous things.

[1]Sing to the LORD á new song,*
for he has done márvelous things.
  [2]With his right hand and his hóly arm*
  has he won for himself the victory. ℟
[3]The LORD has made known his victory;*
his righteousness has he openly shown in the sight óf the nations.
  [4]He remembers his mercy and faithfulness to the hóuse of Israel,*
  and all the ends of the earth have seen the victory óf our God.
[5]Shout with joy to the LORD, áll you lands;*
lift up your voice, rejoice, and sing. ℟

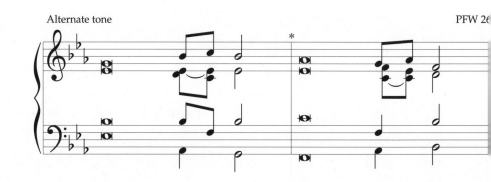

Alternate tone

St. Matthew, Apostle and Evangelist
September 21 | Psalm 119:33-40

Refrain

Anne Krentz Organ

Teach me, O LORD, the way of your stat - utes.

Teach me, O LORD, the way of your stat - utes.

optional introduction

Psalm tone

[33]Teach me, O LORD, the way of your statutes,*
and I shall keep it to the end.
   [34]Give me understanding, and I shall keep your law;*
   I shall keep it with all my heart.
[35]Make me go in the path of your commandments,*
for that is my desire.
   [36]Incline my heart to your decrees*
   and not to unjust gain. ℟
[37]Turn my eyes from watching what is worthless;*
give me life in your ways.
   [38]Fulfill your promise to your servant,*
   which you make to those who fear you.
[39]Turn away the reproach which I dread,*
because your judgments are good.
   [40]Behold, I long for your commandments;*
   in your righteousness preserve my life. ℟

Alternate tone

St. Michael and All Angels

September 29 | Psalm 103:1-5, 20-22

Refrain

Anne Krentz Organ

Bless the LORD, you an - gels

of the LORD.

3 octaves
Handbells used: 8

¹Bless the LORD, Ó my soul,*
and all that is within me, bless his hóly name.
  ²Bless the LORD, Ó my soul,*
  and forget not áll his benefits. R̶
³He forgives áll your sins*
and heals all ýour infirmities;
  ⁴he redeems your life fŕom the grave*
  and crowns you with mercy and lóvingkindness;
⁵he satisfies you wíth good things,*
and your youth is renewed líke an eagle's.
  ²⁰Bless the LORD, you angels of his,
  you mighty ones who ďo his bidding,*
  and hearken to the voice óf his word. R̶
²¹Bless the LORD, all ýou his hosts,*
you ministers of his who ďo his will.
  ²²Bless the LORD, all you works of his,
  in all places of h́is dominion;*
  bless the LORD, Ó my soul. R̶

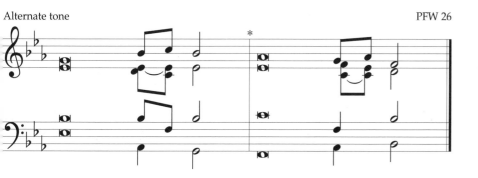

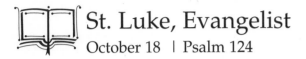

St. Luke, Evangelist
October 18 | Psalm 124

Refrain

Anne Krentz Organ

Our help is in the name of the LORD.

3 octaves
Handbells used: 6

[1]If the LORD had not been ón our side,*
let Israél now say;
   [2]if the LORD had not been ón our side,*
   when enemies rose úp against us,
[3]then would they have swallowed us úp alive*
in their fierce ánger toward us;
   [4]then would the waters have óverwhelmed us*
   and the torrent gone óver us;
[5]then would the ráging waters*
have gone right óver us.
   [6]Blessed be the LORD!*
   He has not given us over to be a prey fór their teeth. R̲
[7]We have escaped like a bird from the snare óf the fowler;*
the snare is broken, and we háve escaped.
   [8]Our help is in the name óf the LORD,*
   the maker of heavén and earth. R̲

Alternate tone

St. Simon and St. Jude, Apostles

October 28 | Psalm 11

Ronald Turner

Refrain

In the LORD have I ta - ken ref - uge.

Psalm tone

[1]In the LORD have I taken refuge;*
how then can you say to me, "Fly away like a bird to the hilltop;
　　[2]for see how the wicked bend the bow and fit their arrows to the string,*
　　to shoot from ambush at the true of heart.
[3]When the foundations are being destroyed,*
what can the righteous do?"
　　[4]The LORD is in his holy temple;*
　　the LORD's throne is in heaven. ℞
[5]His eyes behold the inhabited world;*
his piercing eye weighs our worth.
　　[6]The LORD weighs the righteous as well as the wicked,*
　　but those who delight in violence he abhors.
[7]Upon the wicked he shall rain coals of fire and burning sulphur;*
a scorching wind shall be their lot.
　　[8]For the LORD is righteous; he delights in righteous deeds;*
　　and the just shall see his face. ℞

Alternate tone

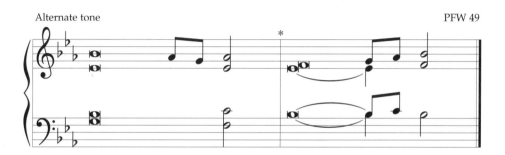

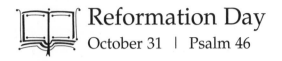

Reformation Day
October 31 | Psalm 46

Refrain

Dale Wood

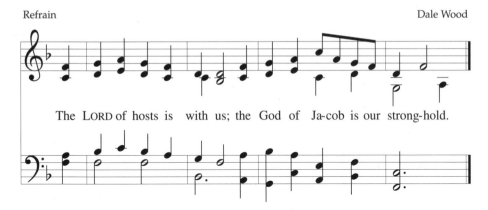

The LORD of hosts is with us; the God of Ja-cob is our strong-hold.

Alternate accompaniment

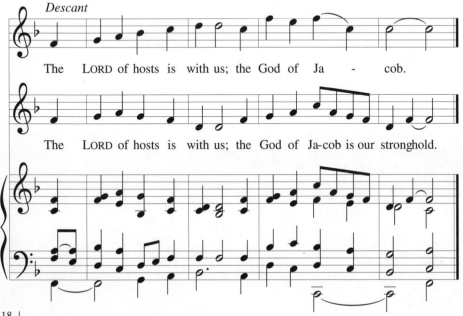

Descant

The LORD of hosts is with us; the God of Ja - cob.

The LORD of hosts is with us; the God of Ja-cob is our stronghold.

¹God is our refúge and strength,*
a very present hélp in trouble.
    ²**Therefore we will not fear, though the éarth be moved,***
    and though the mountains be toppled into the depths óf the sea;
³though its waters ráge and foam,*
and though the mountains tremble át its tumult.
    ⁴**The LORD of hósts is with us;***
    the God of Jacob ís our stronghold. ℞
⁵There is a river whose streams make glad the citý of God,*
the holy habitation of the Most High.
    ⁶**God is in the midst of her; she shall not be óverthrown;***
    God shall help her at the bréak of day.
⁷The nations make much ado, and the kingdoms are shaken;*
God has spoken, and the earth shall melt away.
    ⁸**The LORD of hósts is with us;***
    the God of Jacob ís our stronghold. ℞
⁹Come now and look upon the works óf the LORD,*
what awesome things he has dóne on earth.
    ¹⁰**It is he who makes war to cease in áll the world;***
    he breaks the bow, and shatters the spear, and burns the shields with fire.
¹¹"Be still, then, and know that Í am God;*
I will be exalted among the nations; I will be exalted ín the earth."
    ¹²**The LORD of hósts is with us;***
    the God of Jacob ís our stronghold. ℞

Alternate tone

All Saints Day
November 1 | Psalm 149

Refrain

David Cherwien

Psalm tone

Sing the praise of the Lord in the con - gre - ga - tion of the faith-ful.

Sing the praise of the Lord in the con - gre - ga - tion of the faith-ful.

[1]Hallelujah! Sing to the Lord á new song;*
sing his praise in the congregation óf the faithful.
    [2]Let Israel rejoice ín his maker;*
    let the children of Zion be joyful ín their king.
[3]Let them praise his name ín the dance;*
let them sing praise to him with timbrel and harp.
    [4]For the Lord takes pleasure ín his people*
    and adorns the póor with victory. ℞
[5]Let the faithful réjoice in triumph;*
let them be joyful ón their beds.
    [6]Let the praises of God be ín their throat*
    and a two-edged sword ín their hand;
[7]to wreak vengeance ón the nations*
and punishment ón the peoples;
    [8]to bind their kíngs in chains*
    and their nobles with línks of iron;
[9]to inflict on them the judǵment decreed;*
this is glory for all his faithful people. Hállelujah! ℞

Alternate tone

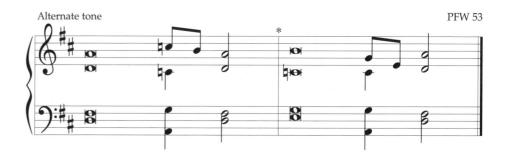

Day of Thanksgiving
Psalm 100

Refrain

David Cherwien

Descant

En - ter the gates of the LORD with thanks- giv - ing.

En - ter the gates of the LORD with thanks- giv - ing.

[1]Be joyful in the LORD, áll you lands;*
serve the LORD with gladness and come before his presence with a song

[2]**Know this: The LORD himsélf is God;***
he himself has made us, and we are his;
we are his people and the sheep óf his pasture. ℟

[3]Enter his gates with thanksgiving; go into his courts with praise;*
give thanks to him and call upón his name.

[4]**For the LORD is good; his mercy is éverlasting;***
and his faithfulness endures from áge to age. ℟

For New Year's Eve, December 31, see The Name of Jesus, p. 96.

PFW 53

PSALM REFRAINS
For Congregational Participation

ngregations that purchase this resource may reproduce the following psalm
rains in congregational bulletins, provided copies are for local use only and not
sale, and that the copyright notice printed below the refrain appears on each copy
de. All other requests for permission must be directed to the publisher.

Third Sunday in Advent

In your midst is the Ho-ly One of Is-ra-el.

Isa. 12:6

Carolyn Jennings

First Sunday in Advent

To you, O Lord, I lift up my soul.

Ps. 25:1

Carolyn Jennings

Fourth Sunday in Advent

The Lord has lift-ed up, has lift-ed up the low-ly.

Luke 1:52

Carolyn Jennings

Second Sunday in Advent

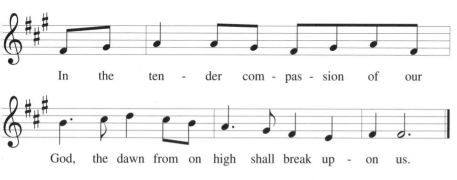

In the ten-der com-pas-sion of our

God, the dawn from on high shall break up-on us.

Luke 1:78

Carolyn Jennings

The Nativity of Our Lord (I) *Christmas Eve*

Let the heav-ens re-joice, and the earth be glad.

Ps. 96:11

Robert Hobby

The Nativity of Our Lord (II) *Christmas Dawn*

Light has sprung up for the righ - teous.

Ps. 97:11

Robert Hobby

The Nativity of Our Lord (III) *Christmas Day*

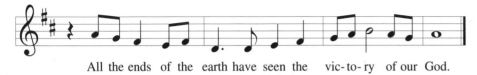

All the ends of the earth have seen the vic-to-ry of our God.

Ps. 98:4

Robert Hobby

First Sunday after Christmas

The splen - dor of the LORD is o - ver earth and heav'n.

Ps. 148:13

Robert Hobby

Second Sunday after Christmas

Wor- ship the LORD, O Je - ru - sa- lem; praise your God, O Zi- on.

Ps. 147:13

Robert Hobby

The Epiphany of Our Lord

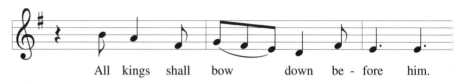

All kings shall bow down be - fore him.

Ps. 72:11

Robert Hobby

The Baptism of Our Lord

First Sunday after the Epiphany

The voice of the LORD is up - on the wa - ters.

Ps. 29:3

Robert Hobby

Second Sunday after the Epiphany

We feast up-on the a-bun-dance of your house, O LORD.

Ps. 36:8

Daniel Kallman

Third Sunday after the Epiphany

The law of the LORD re - vives the soul.

Ps. 19:7

Daniel Kallman

Fourth Sunday after the Epiphany

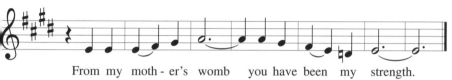

From my moth-er's womb you have been my strength.

Ps. 71:6

Daniel Kallman

Fifth Sunday after the Epiphany

I will bow down toward your ho - ly tem - ple.

Ps. 138:2

Daniel Kallman

Sixth Sunday after the Epiphany

Proper 1

They are like trees plant-ed by streams of wa - ter.

Ps. 1:3

Daniel Kallman

Seventh Sunday after the Epiphany

Proper 2

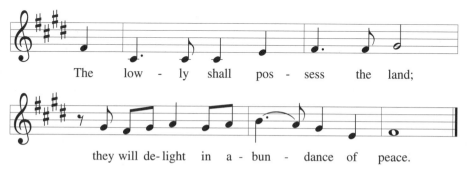

The low - ly shall pos - sess the land;

they will de-light in a - bun - dance of peace.

Ps. 37:12

Daniel Kallman

Eighth Sunday after the Epiphany

Proper 3

The righ-teous shall flour-ish like a palm tree.

Ps. 92:11

Daniel Kallman

Psalm refrain reproduced from *Psalter for Worship, Cycle C* © 1997 Augsburg Fortress.
May be reproduced by permission for local use only.

The Transfiguration of Our Lord

Last Sunday after the Epiphany

Pro - claim the great - ness of the LORD;

wor - ship up - on God's ho - ly hill.

Ps. 99:9

Martin Seltz

Psalm refrain reproduced from *Psalter for Worship, Cycle C* © 1997 Augsburg Fortress.
May be reproduced by permission for local use only.

Ash Wednesday

Have mer - cy on me, O God, ac - cord-ing to your lov - ing - kind-ness.

Ps. 51:1

May Schwarz

Psalm refrain reproduced from *Psalter for Worship, Cycle C* © 1997 Augsburg Fortress.
May be reproduced by permission for local use only.

First Sunday in Lent

God shall charge the an - gels to keep you in all your ways.

Ps. 91:11

Thomas Keeseck

Psalm refrain reproduced from *Psalter for Worship, Cycle C* © 1997 Augsburg Fortress.
May be reproduced by permission for local use only.

Second Sunday in Lent

In the day of trou - ble, the LORD shall keep me safe.

Ps. 27:7

Thomas Keeseck

Psalm refrain reproduced from *Psalter for Worship, Cycle C* © 1997 Augsburg Fortress.
May be reproduced by permission for local use only.

Third Sunday in Lent

O God, ea-ger-ly I seek you; my soul thirsts for you.

Ps. 63:1

Thomas Keeseck

Psalm refrain reproduced from *Psalter for Worship, Cycle C* © 1997 Augsburg Fortress.
May be reproduced by permission for local use only.

Fourth Sunday in Lent

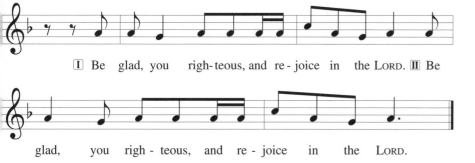

I Be glad, you righ-teous, and re-joice in the LORD. II Be glad, you righ-teous, and re-joice in the LORD.

Ps. 32:12

Thomas Keesecker

Psalm refrain reproduced from *Psalter for Worship, Cycle C* © 1997 Augsburg Fortress.
May be reproduced by permission for local use only.

Fifth Sunday in Lent

Those who sowed with tears will reap with songs of joy.

Ps. 126:6

Thomas Keesecker

Psalm refrain reproduced from *Psalter for Worship, Cycle C* © 1997 Augsburg Fortress.
May be reproduced by permission for local use only.

Sunday of the Passion

Palm Sunday

In - to your hands, O LORD, I com - mend my spir - it.

Ps. 31:5

Robert Buckley Farlee

Psalm refrain reproduced from *Psalter for Worship, Cycle C* © 1997 Augsburg Fortress.
May be reproduced by permission for local use only.

Monday in Holy Week

Your peo - ple take ref - uge un - der the shad-ow of your wings.

Ps. 36:7

Robert Buckley Farlee

Psalm refrain reproduced from *Psalter for Worship, Cycle C* © 1997 Augsburg Fortress.
May be reproduced by permission for local use only.

Tuesday in Holy Week

From my moth - er's womb you have been my strength.

Ps. 71:6

Robert Buckley Farlee

Psalm refrain reproduced from *Psalter for Worship, Cycle C* © 1997 Augsburg Fortress.
May be reproduced by permission for local use only.

Wednesday in Holy Week

Be pleased, O God, to de - liv - er me.

Ps. 70:1

Robert Buckley Farlee

Psalm refrain reproduced from *Psalter for Worship, Cycle C* © 1997 Augsburg Fortress.
May be reproduced by permission for local use only.

Maundy Thursday

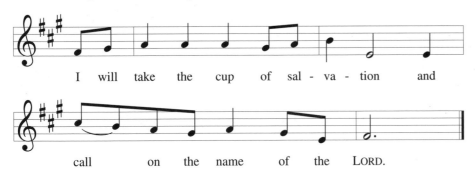

I will take the cup of sal-va-tion and call on the name of the LORD.

Ps. 116:11

Robert Buckley Farlee

Good Friday

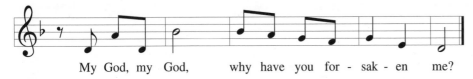

My God, my God, why have you for-sak-en me?

Ps. 22:1

Robert Buckley Farlee

Vigil of Easter • Response 1

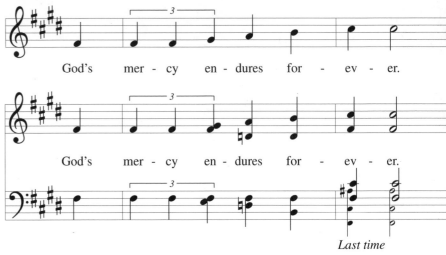

God's mer-cy en-dures for-ev-er.

God's mer-cy en-dures for-ev-er.

Last time

Ps. 136:1b

Thomas Pavlechk

Vigil of Easter • Response 2

The LORD of hosts is with us; the God of Ja-cob is our stronghold.

The LORD of hosts is with us; the God of Ja-cob is our strong-hold.

Ps. 46:4

Dale Wood

Vigil of Easter • Response 3

You will show me the path of life.

You will show me the path of life.

Ps. 16:11

May Schwarz

Vigil of Easter • Response 4

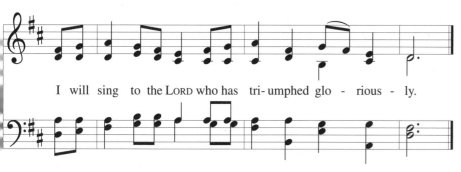

I will sing to the LORD who has tri-umphed glo - rious - ly.

I will sing to the LORD who has tri-umphed glo - rious - ly.

Exod. 15:1

Mark Sedio

Vigil of Easter • Response 5

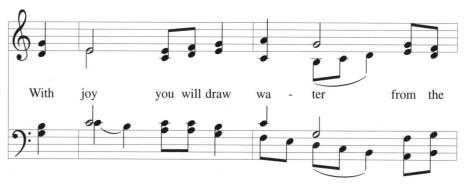

With joy you will draw wa - ter from the wells of sal-va - tion.

With joy you will draw wa - ter from the

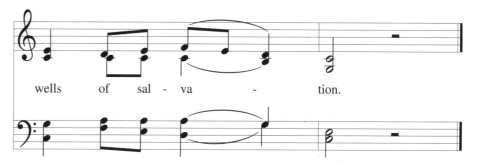

wells of sal - va - tion.

Isa. 12:3

Robert Buckley Farlee

Vigil of Easter • Response 6

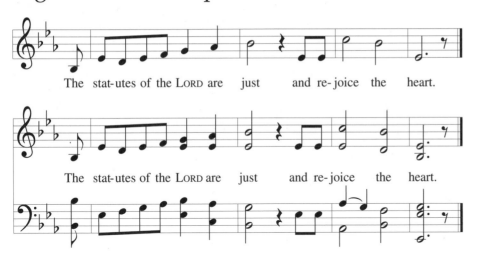

The stat-utes of the LORD are just and re-joice the heart.

The stat-utes of the LORD are just and re-joice the heart.

Ps. 19:8

May Schwarz

Psalm refrain reproduced from *Psalter for Worship, Cycle C* © 1997 Augsburg Fortress.
May be reproduced by permission for local use only.

Vigil of Easter • Response 8

Re - vive me, O LORD, for your name's sake.

Re - vive me, O LORD, for your name's sake.

Ps. 143:11

May Schwarz

Psalm refrain reproduced from *Psalter for Worship, Cycle C* © 1997 Augsburg Fortress.
May be reproduced by permission for local use only.

Vigil of Easter • Response 7

My soul is a - thirst for the liv - ing God.

| To verses | Last time |

My soul is a - thirst for the liv - ing God. God.

Ps. 42:2

Mark Sedio

Psalm refrain reproduced from *Psalter for Worship, Cycle C* © 1997 Augsburg Fortress.
May be reproduced by permission for local use only.

Vigil of Easter • Response 9

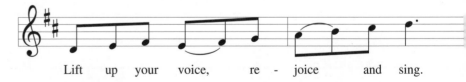

Lift up your voice, re - joice and sing.

Lift up your voice, re - joice and sing.

Ps. 98:5

Mark Sedio

Psalm refrain reproduced from *Psalter for Worship, Cycle C* © 1997 Augsburg Fortress.
May be reproduced by permission for local use only.

Vigil of Easter • Response 10

Jonah 2:9

Robert Buckley Farlee

Vigil of Easter • Response 11

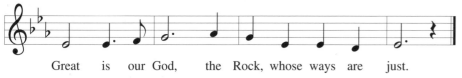

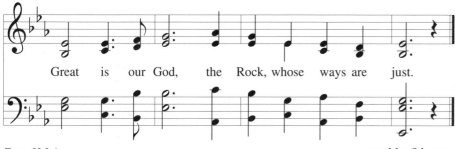

Deut. 32:3-4

arr. May Schwarz

Vigil of Easter • Response 12

Song of the Three Young Men 35b

Mark Sedio

Vigil of Easter • Psalm 114

Ps. 114:7

Robert Buckley Farlee

The Resurrection of Our Lord

On this day the LORD has act-ed; we will rejoice and be glad in it.

Ps. 118:24

Carl Schalk

Psalm refrain reproduced from *Psalter for Worship, Cycle C* © 1997 Augsburg Fortress.
May be reproduced by permission for local use only.

Second Sunday of Easter

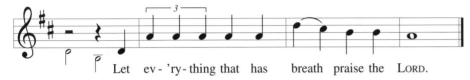

Let ev - 'ry-thing that has breath praise the LORD.

Ps. 150:6

Carl Schalk

Psalm refrain reproduced from *Psalter for Worship, Cycle C* © 1997 Augsburg Fortress.
May be reproduced by permission for local use only.

Third Sunday of Easter

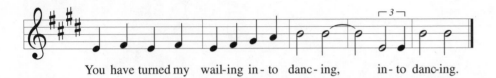

You have turned my wail-ing in - to danc - ing, in - to danc-ing.

Ps. 30:12

Carl Schalk

Psalm refrain reproduced from *Psalter for Worship, Cycle C* © 1997 Augsburg Fortress.
May be reproduced by permission for local use only.

Fourth Sunday of Easter

The LORD is my shepherd; I shall not be in want.

Ps. 23:1

Carl Schalk

Psalm refrain reproduced from *Psalter for Worship, Cycle C* © 1997 Augsburg Fortress.
May be reproduced by permission for local use only.

Fifth Sunday of Easter

The splendor of the LORD is o - ver earth and heav'n.

Ps. 148:13

Carl Schalk

Psalm refrain reproduced from *Psalter for Worship, Cycle C* © 1997 Augsburg Fortress.
May be reproduced by permission for local use only.

Sixth Sunday of Easter

Let the na - tions be glad and sing for joy.

Ps. 67:4

Carl Schalk

Psalm refrain reproduced from *Psalter for Worship, Cycle C* © 1997 Augsburg Fortress.
May be reproduced by permission for local use only.

The Ascension of Our Lord

God has gone up with a shout; sing prais-es to God, sing praises.

Ps. 47:5

Walter Pelz

The Day of Pentecost

Send forth your Spir-it and re - new the face of the earth.

Ps. 104:31

Carl Schalk

Seventh Sunday of Easter

Re - joice in the LORD, you righ - teous.

Ps. 97:12

Carl Schalk

The Holy Trinity
First Sunday after Pentecost

Your maj - es - ty is praised a - bove the heav-ens.

Ps. 8:2

Valerie Shields

Vigil of Pentecost

The LORD is our help and our shield.

Ps. 33:20

Robert Buckley Farlee

Sunday between May 28 and June 4
Proper 4

De - clare the glo-ry of the LORD a-mong the na-tions.

Ps. 96:3

Valerie Shields

Sunday between June 5 and 11

Proper 5

My God, I cried out to you, and you re-stored me to health.

Ps. 30:2

Valerie Shields

Sunday between June 12 and 18

Proper 6

Then you for-gave me the guilt of my sin.

Ps. 32:6

Valerie Shields

Sunday between June 19 and 25

Proper 7

In the midst of the con-gre-ga-tion I will praise you.

Ps. 22:21

Valerie Shields

Sunday between June 26 and July 2

Proper 8

I have set the Lord al - ways be-fore me.

Ps. 16:8

Valerie Shields

Sunday between July 3 and 9

Proper 9

God holds our souls, our souls in life.

Ps. 66:8

Valerie Shields

Sunday between July 10 and 16

Proper 10

Show me your ways, O Lord, and teach me your paths.

Ps. 25:3

Valerie Shields

Sunday between July 17 and 23

Proper 11

Who may a-bide up-on your ho-ly hill? Who-ev-er leads a blame-less life and does what is right.

Ps. 15:1-2

John Paradowski

Psalm refrain reproduced from *Psalter for Worship, Cycle C* © 1997 Augsburg Fortress.
May be reproduced by permission for local use only.

Sunday between July 24 and 30

Proper 12

Your love en-dures for-ev-er; do not a-ban-don the works of your hands.

Ps. 138:9

John Paradowski

Psalm refrain reproduced from *Psalter for Worship, Cycle C* © 1997 Augsburg Fortress.
May be reproduced by permission for local use only.

Sunday between July 31 and August 6

Proper 13

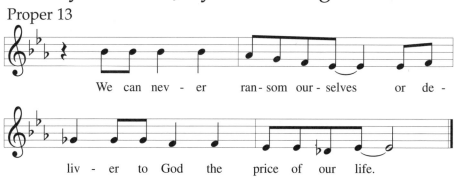

We can nev-er ran-som our-selves or de-liv-er to God the price of our life.

Ps. 49:6

John Paradowski

Psalm refrain reproduced from *Psalter for Worship, Cycle C* © 1997 Augsburg Fortress.
May be reproduced by permission for local use only.

Sunday between August 7 and 13

Proper 14

Let your lov-ing-kind-ness be up-on us, as we have put our trust in you.

Ps. 33:22

John Paradowski

Psalm refrain reproduced from *Psalter for Worship, Cycle C* © 1997 Augsburg Fortress.
May be reproduced by permission for local use only.

Sunday between August 14 and 20

Proper 15

A - rise, O God, and rule the earth.

Ps. 82:8

John Paradowski

Sunday between August 21 and 27

Proper 16

The LORD crowns you with mer-cy and lov - ing - kind-ness.

Ps. 103:4

John Paradowski

Sunday between August 28 and September 3

Proper 17

The righ-teous are mer-ci-ful and full of com - pas-sion.

Ps. 112:4

John Paradowski

Sunday between September 4 and 10

Proper 18

Their de - light is in the law of the LORD.

Ps. 1:2

Dorothy Christophers

Sunday between September 11 and 17

Proper 19

Have mer-cy on me, O God, ac -

cord - ing to your lov - ing kind - ness.

Ps. 51:1

Dorothy Christophers

Sunday between September 18 and 24

Proper 20

The LORD lifts up the poor from the ash - es.

Ps. 113:6

Dorothy Christophers

Sunday between September 25 and October 1
Proper 21

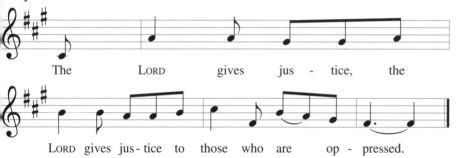

The Lord gives jus-tice, the Lord gives jus-tice to those who are op-pressed.

Ps. 146:6

Dorothy Christopherson

Sunday between October 2 and 8
Proper 22

Com-mit your way to the Lord; put your trust in the Lord.

Ps. 37:5

Dorothy Christopherson

Sunday between October 9 and 15
Proper 23

I will give thanks, I will give thanks to the Lord with my whole heart.

Ps. 111:1

Dorothy Christopherson

Sunday between October 16 and 22
Proper 24

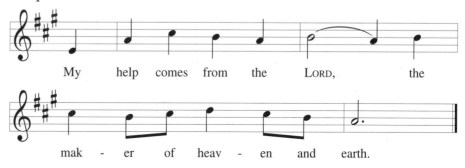

My help comes from the Lord, the mak-er of heav-en and earth.

Ps. 121:2

Dorothy Christopherson

Sunday between October 23 and 29
Proper 25

Hap-py are the peo-ple whose strength is in you.

Ps. 84:4

David Cherwien

Psalm refrain reproduced from *Psalter for Worship, Cycle C* © 1997 Augsburg Fortress.
May be reproduced by permission for local use only.

Sunday between October 30 and November 5
Proper 26

All the faith-ful will make their prayers to you in time of trou-ble.

Ps. 32:7

David Cherwien

Psalm refrain reproduced from *Psalter for Worship, Cycle C* © 1997 Augsburg Fortress.
May be reproduced by permission for local use only.

Sunday between November 6 and 12
Proper 27

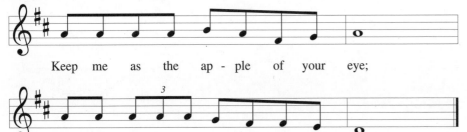

Keep me as the ap-ple of your eye;

hide me un-der the shad-ow of your wings.

Ps. 17:8

David Cherwien

Psalm refrain reproduced from *Psalter for Worship, Cycle C* © 1997 Augsburg Fortress.
May be reproduced by permission for local use only.

Sunday between November 13 and 19
Proper 28

In righ-teous-ness shall the LORD judge the world.

Ps. 98:10

David Cherwi

Psalm refrain reproduced from *Psalter for Worship, Cycle C* © 1997 Augsburg Fortress.
May be reproduced by permission for local use only.

Christ the King
Sunday between November 20 and 26 | Proper 29

I will be ex-alt-ed a-mong the na-tions.

Ps. 46:11

David Cherwi

Psalm refrain reproduced from *Psalter for Worship, Cycle C* © 1997 Augsburg Fortress.
May be reproduced by permission for local use only.

St. Andrew, Apostle
November 30

Their sound has gone out in-to all lands.

Ps. 19:4

Thomas Pavlechk

Psalm refrain reproduced from *Psalter for Worship, Cycle C* © 1997 Augsburg Fortress.
May be reproduced by permission for local use only.

St. Thomas, Apostle

December 21

God's mer-cy en-dures for - ev - er.

Ps. 136:1b

Thomas Pavlechko

St. Stephen, Deacon and Martyr

December 26

I call up-on you, O God, for you will an-swer me.

Ps. 17:6

Thomas Pavlechko

St. John, Apostle and Evangelist

December 27

Pre-cious in your sight, O LORD, is the death of your ser-vants.

Ps. 116:13

Thomas Pavlechko

The Holy Innocents

December 28

We have es - caped like a bird from the snare of the fowl - er.

Ps. 124:7

Thomas Pavlechko

The Name of Jesus

January 1

How ex - al - ted is your name in all the world, all the world,

how ex - al - ted is your name in all the world!

Ps. 8:1

Michael Hassell

The Confession of St. Peter

January 18

My God, my rock, you are wor-thy of praise.

Ps. 18:2

Thomas Pavlechko

The Conversion of St. Paul

January 25

Let all the peo-ples praise you, O God.

Ps. 67:3

Thomas Pavlechko

The Presentation of Our Lord

February 2

How dear to me is your dwell - ing, O LORD.

Ps. 84:1

arr. Thomas Pavlechko

St. Matthias, Apostle

February 24

I am bound by the vow I made to you, O God.

Ps. 56:11

Thomas Pavlechko

The Annunciation of Our Lord

March 25

I love to do your will, O my God, O my God.

Ps. 40:9

John Folkenir

St. Mark, Evangelist

April 25

I will con-fess you a-mong the peo-ples, O LORD.

Ps. 57:9

Ronald Turn

St. Philip and St. James, Apostles

May 1

Save us, save us for the sake of your stead-fast love.

Ps. 44:26

Ronald Turner

The Visitation

May 31

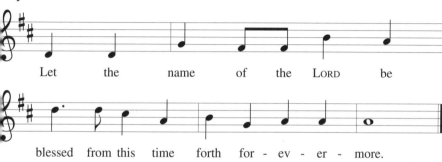

Let the name of the LORD be

blessed from this time forth for - ev - er - more.

Ps. 113:2

Carolyn Jennings

St. Barnabas, Apostle

June 11

Hap-py are they who fear the LORD, who fear the LORD.

Ps. 112:1

Ronald Turner

The Nativity of St. John the Baptist

June 24

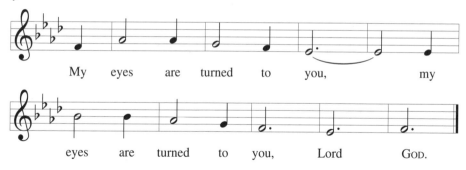

My eyes are turned to you, my

eyes are turned to you, Lord GOD.

Ps. 141:8

Ronald Turner

St. Peter and St. Paul, Apostles

June 29

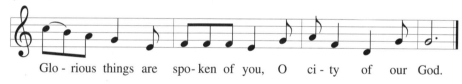

Glo - rious things are spo-ken of you, O ci - ty of our God.

Ps. 87:2

Anne Krentz Organ

St. Mary Magdalene

July 22

I will speak of all your works in the gates of the cit - y of Zi - on.

Ps. 73:29

Carolyn Jennings

St. James the Elder, Apostle

July 25

God is my shield, my shield and de- fense.

Ps. 7:11

Ronald Turner

Psalm refrain reproduced from *Psalter for Worship, Cycle C* © 1997 Augsburg Fortress.
May be reproduced by permission for local use only.

Mary, Mother of Our Lord

August 15

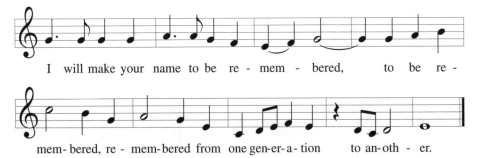

I will make your name to be re- mem - bered, to be re -

mem- bered, re - mem-bered from one gen-er- a- tion to an-oth - er.

Ps. 45:18

Carolyn Jennings

Psalm refrain reproduced from *Psalter for Worship, Cycle C* © 1997 Augsburg Fortress.
May be reproduced by permission for local use only.

St. Bartholomew, Apostle

August 24

The words of the LORD are pure.

Ps. 12:6

Anne Krentz Organ

Psalm refrain reproduced from *Psalter for Worship, Cycle C* © 1997 Augsburg Fortress.
May be reproduced by permission for local use only.

Holy Cross Day

September 14

The LORD has done mar- vel- ous things.

Ps. 98:1

Anne Krentz Or

Psalm refrain reproduced from *Psalter for Worship, Cycle C* © 1997 Augsburg Fortress.
May be reproduced by permission for local use only.

St. Matthew, Apostle

September 21

Teach me, O LORD, the way of your stat- utes.

Ps. 119:33

Anne Krentz Or

Psalm refrain reproduced from *Psalter for Worship, Cycle C* © 1997 Augsburg Fortress.
May be reproduced by permission for local use only.

St. Michael and All Angels

September 29

Bless the LORD, you an - gels of the LORD.

Ps. 103:20

Anne Krentz Or

Psalm refrain reproduced from *Psalter for Worship, Cycle C* © 1997 Augsburg Fortress.
May be reproduced by permission for local use only.

St. Luke, Evangelist

October 18

Our help is in the name of the LORD.

Ps. 124:8

Anne Krentz Organ

St. Simon and St. Jude

October 28

In the LORD have I ta - ken ref - uge.

Ps. 11:1

Ronald Turner

Reformation Day

October 31

The LORD of hosts is with us; the God of Ja - cob is our stronghold.

Ps. 46:4

Dale Wood

All Saints Day

November 1

Sing the praise of the LORD in the con - gre - ga - tion of the faith-ful.

Ps. 149:1

David Cherwien

New Year's Eve

December 31

How ex - al - ted is your name in all the world, all the world,

how ex - al - ted is your name in all the world!

Ps. 8:1

Michael Hassell

Day of Thanksgiving

En - ter the gates of the LORD with thanks - giv - ing.

Ps. 100:3

David Cherwien

PSALM TONES
For Congregational Participation

Congregations that purchase this resource may reproduce the following psalm tones in congregational bulletins, provided copies are for local use only and not for sale, and that the copyright notice printed below the refrain appears on each copy made. All other requests for permission must be directed to the publisher.

LBW 1 (E)

LBW 1 (C)

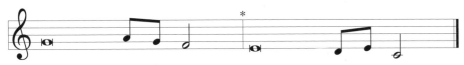

LBW 2 (C)

LBW 1 (D)

LBW 2 (D)

LBW 1 (E♭)

LBW 2 (E)

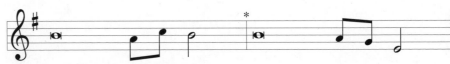

LBW 3 (C)

LBW 3 (D)

LBW 3 (E♭)

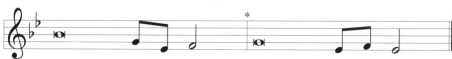

LBW 3 (E)

LBW 3 (F)

LBW 4 (F)

LBW 5 (D)

LBW 5 (E)

LBW 5 (F♯)

LBW 5 (G)

LBW 9 (D)

LBW 9 (E♭)

LBW 9 (E)

LBW 10 (E)

LBW 10 (F♯)

LBW 10 (G)

PFW 22 (C)

PFW 25 (D)

PFW 22 (D)

PFW 26 (E♭)

PFW 22 (E♭)

PFW 34 (F)

PFW 24 (E♭)

PFW 36 (D)

PFW 37 (F)

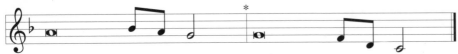

Psalm tone reproduced from *Psalter for Worship, Cycle C,* © 1997 Augsburg Fortress. May be reproduced by permission for local use only.

PFW 40 (D)

Psalm tone reproduced from *Psalter for Worship, Cycle C,* © 1997 Augsburg Fortress. May be reproduced by permission for local use only.

PFW 42 (F#)

Psalm tone reproduced from *Psalter for Worship, Cycle C* © 1997 Augsburg Fortress. May be reproduced by permission for local use only.

PFW 43 (F#)

Psalm tone reproduced from *Psalter for Worship, Cycle C* © 1997 Augsburg Fortress. May be reproduced by permission for local use only.

PFW 43 (G)

Psalm tone reproduced from *Psalter for Worship, Cycle C* © 1997 Augsburg Fortress. May be reproduced by permission for local use only.

PFW 44 (E♭)

Psalm tone reproduced from *Psalter for Worship, Cycle C* © 1997 Augsburg Fortress. May be reproduced by permission for local use only.

PFW 44 (F)

Psalm tone reproduced from *Psalter for Worship, Cycle C* © 1997 Augsburg Fortress. May be reproduced by permission for local use only.

PFW 45 (F)

Psalm tone reproduced from *Psalter for Worship, Cycle C* © 1997 Augsburg Fortress. May be reproduced by permission for local use only.

PFW 46 (D)

Psalm tone reproduced from *Psalter for Worship, Cycle C* © 1997 Augsburg Fortress. May be reproduced by permission for local use only.

PFW 47 (F)

Psalm tone reproduced from *Psalter for Worship, Cycle C* © 1997 Augsburg Fortress. May be reproduced by permission for local use only.

PFW 48 (E♭)

Psalm tone reproduced from *Psalter for Worship, Cycle C* © 1997 Augsburg Fortress. May be reproduced by permission for local use only.

PFW 49 (C)

Psalm tone reproduced from *Psalter for Worship, Cycle C* © 1997 Augsburg Fortress. May be reproduced by permission for local use only.

PFW 49 (D)

Psalm tone reproduced from *Psalter for Worship, Cycle C* © 1997 Augsburg Fortress. May be reproduced by permission for local use only.

PFW 49 (E♭)

Psalm tone reproduced from *Psalter for Worship, Cycle C* © 1997 Augsburg Fortress. May be reproduced by permission for local use only.

PFW 49 (E)

Psalm tone reproduced from *Psalter for Worship, Cycle C* © 1997 Augsburg Fortress. May be reproduced by permission for local use only.

PFW 50 (D)

Psalm tone reproduced from *Psalter for Worship, Cycle C* © 1997 Augsburg Fortress. May be reproduced by permission for local use only.

PFW 50 (E)

Psalm tone reproduced from *Psalter for Worship, Cycle C* © 1997 Augsburg Fortress. May be reproduced by permission for local use only.

PFW 51 (C)

Psalm tone reproduced from *Psalter for Worship, Cycle C* © 1997 Augsburg Fortress. May be reproduced by permission for local use only.

PFW 51 (D)

Psalm tone reproduced from *Psalter for Worship, Cycle C* © 1997 Augsburg Fortress. May be reproduced by permission for local use only.

PFW 51 (E♭)

Psalm tone reproduced from *Psalter for Worship, Cycle C* © 1997 Augsburg Fortress. May be reproduced by permission for local use only.

PFW 51 (E)

Psalm tone reproduced from *Psalter for Worship, Cycle C* © 1997 Augsburg Fortress. May be reproduced by permission for local use only.

PFW 52 (E)

Psalm tone reproduced from *Psalter for Worship, Cycle C* © 1997 Augsburg Fortress. May be reproduced by permission for local use only.

PFW 52 (F#)

Psalm tone reproduced from *Psalter for Worship, Cycle C* © 1997 Augsburg Fortress. May be reproduced by permission for local use only.

PFW 53 (C)

Psalm tone reproduced from *Psalter for Worship, Cycle C* © 1997 Augsburg Fortress. May be reproduced by permission for local use only.

PFW 53 (D)

Psalm tone reproduced from *Psalter for Worship, Cycle C* © 1997 Augsburg Fortress. May be reproduced by permission for local use only.

Index to the Revised Common Lectionary Psalter

The following index lists, in numerical order, the psalms appointed by the Revised Common Lectionary for the three year cycle. Psalms noted here for the season after Pentecost are those identified with the typological (Gospel-correlated) Old Testament readings. The list also includes the refrain for each psalm, as well as the psalms and refrains for days not covered by the RCL, as appointed in *With One Voice: Leaders Edition. Lutheran Book of Worship* and *Book of Common Prayer* versification is used.

Psalm	Day	Refrain
1	Epiphany 6 C	They are like trees planted by streams of water. (3)
1	Easter 7 B	The LORD knows the way of the righteous. (6)
1	Proper 18 C	Their delight is in the law of the LORD. (2)
1	Proper 25 A	Their delight is in the law of the LORD. (2)
2	Transfiguration A	You are my son; this day have I begotten you. (7)
4	Easter 3 B	The LORD does wonders for the faithful. (3)
7:1-11	St. James the Elder	God is my shield and defense. (11)
8	Name of Jesus	How exalted is your name in all the world! (1)
8	New Year's Eve	How exalted is your name in all the world! (1)
8	Holy Trinity A	How exalted is your name in all the world! (1)
8	Holy Trinity C	Your majesty is praised above the heavens. (2)
8	Proper 22 B	You adorn us with glory and honor. (6)
11	St. Simon and St. Jude	In the LORD have I taken refuge. (1)
12	St. Bartholomew	The words of the LORD are pure. (6)
15	Epiphany 4 A	LORD, who may abide upon your holy hill? (1)
15	Proper 17 B	LORD, who may dwell in your tabernacle? (1)
15	Proper 11 C	Who may abide upon your holy hill? Whoever leads a blameless life and does what is right. (1-2)
16	Easter 2 A	In your presence there is fullness of joy. (11)
16	Vigil of Easter	You will show me the path of life. (11)
16	Proper 28 B	My heart is glad and my spirit rejoices; my body shall rest in hope. (9)
16	Proper 8 C	I have set the LORD always before me. (8)
17:1-9	Proper 27 C	Keep me as the apple of your eye; hide me under the shadow of your wings. (8)
17:1-9, 16	St. Stephen	I call upon you, O God, for you will answer me. (6)
18:1-7, 17-20	Confession of St. Peter	My God, my rock, you are worthy of praise. (2)
19	Vigil of Easter	The statutes of the LORD are just and rejoice the heart. (8)
19	Epiphany 3 C	The law of the LORD revives the soul. (7)
19	Lent 3 B	The commandment of the LORD gives light to the eyes. (8)
19:1-6	St. Andrew	Their sound has gone out into all lands. (4)

Psalm	Day	Refrain
19:7-14	Proper 21 B	The commandment of the LORD gives light to the eyes. (8)
22	Good Friday	My God, my God, why have you forsaken me? (1)
22:18-27	Proper 7 C	In the midst of the congregation I will praise you. (21)
22:22-30	Lent 2 B	All the ends of the earth shall remember and turn to the LORD. (26)
22:24-30	Easter 5 B	All the ends of the earth shall remember and turn to the LORD. (26)
23	Lent 4 A	You have anointed my head with oil. (5)
23	Proper 23 A	You spread a table before me, and my cup is running over. (5)
23	Easter 4 ABC	The LORD is my shepherd; I shall not be in want. (1)
23	Proper 11 B	The LORD is my shepherd; I shall not be in want. (1)
24	All Saints B	They shall receive a blessing from the God of their salvation. (5)
24:7-10	Presentation	Lift up your heads, O gates, and the King of glory shall come in. (7)
25:1-8	Proper 21 A	Remember, O LORD, your compassion and love. (5)
25:1-9	Lent 1 B	Your paths are love and faithfulness to those who keep your covenant. (9)
25:1-9	Advent 1 C	To you, O LORD, I lift up my soul. (1)
25:1-9	Proper 10 C	Show me your ways, O LORD, and teach me your paths. (3)
26:1-8	Proper 17 A	Your love is before my eyes; I have walked faithfully with you. (3)
27	Lent 2 C	In the day of trouble, the LORD shall keep me safe. (7)
27:1, 5-13	Epiphany 3 A	The LORD is my light and my salvation. (1)
29	Baptism of Our Lord	The voice of the LORD is upon the waters. (3)
29	Holy Trinity B	Worship the LORD in the beauty of holiness. (2)
30	Easter 3 C	You have turned my wailing into dancing. (12)
30	Epiphany 6 B	My God, I cried out to you, and you restored me to health. (2)
30	Proper 5 C	My God, I cried out to you, and you restored me to health. (2)
30	Proper 8 B	I will exalt you, O LORD, because you have lifted me up. (1)
31:1-5, 19-24	Proper 4 A	Be my strong rock, a castle to keep me safe. (3)
31:1-5, 15-16	Easter 5 A	Into your hands, O LORD, I commend my spirit. (5)
31:9-16	Sunday of the Passion	Into your hands, O LORD, I commend my spirit. (5)
32	Lent 1 A	Mercy embraces those who trust in the LORD. (11)
32	Lent 4 C	Be glad, you righteous, and rejoice in the LORD. (12)
32	Proper 6 C	Then you forgave me the guilt of my sin. (6)
32:1-8	Proper 26 C	All the faithful will make their prayers to you in time of trouble. (7)
33:12-22	Proper 14 C	Let your lovingkindness be upon us, as we have put our trust in you. (22)
33:12-22	Vigil of Pentecost	The LORD is our help and our shield. (20)
34:1-8	Proper 14 B	Taste and see that the LORD is good. (8)

Psalm	Day	Refrain
34:1-10, 22	All Saints A	Fear the LORD, you saints of the LORD. (9)
34:9-14	Proper 15 B	Those who seek the LORD lack nothing that is good. (10)
34:15-22	Proper 16 B	The eyes of the LORD are upon the righteous. (15)
36:5-10	Epiphany 2 C	We feast upon the abundance of your house, O LORD. (8)
36:5-11	Monday in Holy Week	Your people take refuge under the shadow of your wings. (7)
37:1-10	Proper 22 C	Commit your way to the LORD; put your trust in the LORD. (5)
37:1-12, 41-42	Epiphany 7 C	The lowly shall possess the land; they will delight in the abundance of peace. (12)
40:1-12	Epiphany 2 A	I love to do your will, O my God. (9)
40:5-11	Annunciation	I love to do your will, O my God. (9)
41	Epiphany 7 B	Heal me, for I have sinned against you. (4)
42–43	Vigil of Easter	My soul is athirst for the living God. (42:2)
43	Proper 26 A	Send out your light and truth that they may lead me. (3)
44:1-3, 20-26	St. Philip and St. James	Save us for the sake of your steadfast love. (26)
45	Annunciation	I will make your name to be remembered from one generation to another. (18)
45:11-16	Mary, Mother of Our Lord	I will make your name to be remembered from one generation to another. (18)
46	Christ the King C	I will be exalted among the nations. (11)
46	Vigil of Easter	The LORD of hosts is with us; the God of Jacob is our stronghold. (4)
46	Reformation Day	The LORD of hosts is with us; the God of Jacob is our stronghold. (4)
47	Ascension	God has gone up with a shout. (5)
49:1-11	Proper 13 C	We can never ransom ourselves or deliver to God the price of our life. (6)
50:1-6	Transfiguration B	Out of Zion, perfect in beauty, God shines forth in glory. (2)
50:7-15	Proper 5 A	To those who keep in my way will I show the salvation of God. (24)
51:1-13	Lent 5 B	Create in me a clean heart, O God. (11)
51:1-11	Proper 19 C	Have mercy on me, O God, according to your lovingkindness. (1)
51:1-18	Ash Wednesday	Have mercy on me, O God, according to your lovingkindness. (1)
54	Proper 20 B	God is my helper; it is the LORD who sustains my life. (4)
56	St. Matthias	I am bound by the vow I made to you, O God. (11)
57	St. Mark	I will confess you among the peoples, O LORD. (9)
62:6-14	Epiphany 3 B	In God is my safety and my honor. (8)
63:1-8	Lent 3 C	O God, eagerly I seek you; my soul thirsts for you. (1)
65	Thanksgiving A	You crown the year with your goodness, and your paths overflow with plenty. (12)
65:[1-8] 9-14	Proper 10 A	Your paths overflow with plenty. (12)
66:1-8	Proper 9 C	God holds our souls in life. (8)
66:7-18	Easter 6 A	Be joyful in God, all you lands. (1)

Psalm	Day	Refrain
67	Proper 15 A	Let all the peoples praise you, O God. (3)
67	Conversion of St. Paul	Let all the peoples praise you, O God. (3)
67	Easter 6 C	Let the nations be glad and sing for joy. (4)
68:1-10, 33-36	Easter 7 A	Sing to God, who rides upon the heavens. (4)
69:8-11 [12-17] 18-20	Proper 7 A	Answer me, O God, for your love is kind. (18)
70	Proper 27 A	You are my helper and my deliverer; O LORD, do not tarry. (6)
70	Wednesday in Holy Week	Be pleased, O God, to deliver me. (1)
71:1-6	Epiphany 4 C	From my mother's womb you have been my strength. (6)
71:1-14	Tuesday in Holy Week	From my mother's womb you have been my strength. (6)
72:1-7, 10-14	Epiphany	All kings shall bow down before him. (11)
72:1-7, 18-19	Advent 2 A	In his time the righteous shall flourish. (7)
73:23-29	St. Mary Magdalene	I will speak of all your works in the gates of the city of Zion. (29)
78:1-2, 34-38	Holy Cross Day	God was their rock and the Most High God their redeemer. (35)
78:23-29	Proper 13 B	The LORD rained down manna upon them to eat. (24)
80:1-7, 16-18	Advent 4 A	Show the light of your countenance, and we shall be saved. (7)
80:1-7, 16-18	Advent 1 B	Show the light of your countenance, and we shall be saved. (7)
80:1-7	Advent 4 C	Show the light of your countenance, and we shall be saved. (7)
80:7-14	Proper 22 A	Look down from heaven, O God; behold and tend this vine. (14)
81:1-10	Proper 4 B	Raise a loud shout to the God of Jacob. (1)
82	Proper 15 C	Arise, O God, and rule the earth. (8)
84	Presentation	How dear to me is your dwelling, O LORD. (1)
84:1-6	Proper 25 C	Happy are the people whose strength is in you. (4)
85:1-2, 8-13	Advent 2 B	Righteousness and peace shall go before the LORD. (13)
85:8-13	Proper 14 A	I will listen to what the LORD God is saying. (8)
85:8-13	Proper 10 B	I will listen to what the LORD God is saying. (8)
86:11-17	Proper 11 A	Teach me your way, O LORD, and I will walk in your truth. (11)
87:1-2, 4-6	St. Peter and St. Paul	Glorious things are spoken of you, O city of our God. (2)
89:1-4, 15-18	Proper 8 A	Your love, O LORD, forever will I sing. (1)
89:1-4, 19-26	Advent 4 B	Your love, O LORD, forever will I sing. (1)
90:1-8 [9-11] 12	Proper 28 A	So teach us to number our days that we may apply our hearts to wisdom. (12)
90:12-17	Proper 23 B	So teach us to number our days that we may apply our hearts to wisdom. (12)
91:1-2, 9-16	Lent 1 C	God shall charge the angels to keep you in all your ways. (11)
91:9-16	Proper 24 B	You have made the LORD your refuge, and the Most High your habitation. (9)
92:1-4, 11-14	Epiphany 8/Proper 3 C	The righteous shall flourish like a palm tree. (11)

Psalm	Day	Refrain
92:1-4, 11-14	Proper 6 B	The righteous shall spread abroad like a cedar of Lebanon. (11)
93	Christ the King B	Ever since the world began, your throne has been established. (3)
93	Ascension	Ever since the world began, your throne has been established. (3)
95	Lent 3 A	Let us shout for joy to the rock of our salvation. (1)
95:1-7a	Christ the King A	We are the people of God's pasture and the sheep of God's hand. (7)
96	Christmas Eve	Let the heavens rejoice and the earth be glad. (11)
96:1-9	Proper 4 C	Declare the glory of the LORD among the nations. (3)
96:1-9 [10-13]	Proper 24 A	Ascribe to the LORD honor and power. (7)
97	Christmas Dawn	Light has sprung up for the righteous. (11)
97	Easter 7 C	Rejoice in the LORD, you righteous. (12)
98	Christmas Day	All the ends of the earth have seen the victory of our God. (4)
98	Vigil of Easter	Lift up your voice, rejoice and sing. (5)
98	Easter 6 B	Shout with joy to the LORD, all you lands. (5)
98	Proper 28 C	In righteousness shall the LORD judge the world. (10)
98:1-5	Holy Cross Day	The LORD has done marvelous things. (1)
99	Transfiguration AC	Proclaim the greatness of the LORD; worship upon God's holy hill. (9)
100	Proper 6 A	We are God's people and the sheep of God's pasture. (2)
100	Thanksgiving C	Enter the gates of the LORD with thanksgiving. (3)
103:1-5, 20-22	St. Michael and All Angels	Bless the LORD, you angels of the LORD. (20)
103:1-8	Proper 16 C	The LORD crowns you with mercy and lovingkindness. (4)
103:[1-7] 8-13	Proper 19 A	The LORD is full of compassion and mercy. (8)
103:1-13, 22	Epiphany 8/Proper 3 B	The LORD is full of compassion and mercy. (8)
104:25-35, 37	Day of Pentecost	Alleluia (37b) or Send forth your Spirit and renew the face of the earth. (31)
107:1-3, 17-22	Lent 4 B	The LORD delivered them from their distress. (19)
107:1-3, 23-32	Proper 7 B	God stilled the storm and quieted the waves of the sea. (29)
111	Epiphany 4 B	The fear of the LORD is the beginning of wisdom. (10)
111	Proper 23 C	I will give thanks to the LORD with my whole heart. (1)
112	St. Barnabas	Happy are they who fear the LORD. (1)
112	Proper 17 C	The righteous are merciful and full of compassion. (4)
112:1-9 [10]	Epiphany 5 A	Light shines in the darkness for the upright. (4)
113	Proper 20 C	The LORD lifts up the poor from the ashes. (6)
113	Visitation	Let the name of the LORD be blessed from this time forth forevermore. (2)
114	Easter Evening	Hallelujah. (1)
114	Vigil of Easter	Tremble, O earth, at the presence of the LORD. (7)

Psalm	Day	Refrain
116:1-3, 10-17	Easter 3 A	I will call upon the name of the LORD. (11)
116:1, 10-17	Maundy Thursday	I will take the cup of salvation and call on the name of the LORD. (11)
116:1-8	Proper 19 B	I will walk in the presence of the LORD. (8)
116:10-17	St. John	Precious in your sight, O LORD, is the death of your servants. (13)
118:1-2, 14-24	Easter Day	On this day the LORD has acted; we will rejoice and be glad in it. (24)
118:1-2, 19-29	Sunday of the Passion	Blessed is he who comes in the name of the LORD. (26)
118:14-29	Easter 2 C	This is the LORD's doing and it is marvelous in our eyes. (23)
119:1-8	Epiphany 6 A	Happy are they who walk in the law of the LORD. (1)
119:1-8	Proper 26 B	Happy are they who seek the LORD with all their hearts. (2)
119:9-16	Lent 5 B	I treasure your promise in my heart. (11)
119:33-40	Epiphany 7 A	Teach me, O LORD, the way of your statutes. (33)
119:33-40	St. Matthew	Teach me, O LORD, the way of your statutes. (33)
119:33-40	Proper 18 A	I desire the path of your commandments. (35)
119:129-136	Proper 12 A	When your word goes forth, it gives light and understanding. (130)
121	Lent 2 A	It is the LORD who watches over you. (5)
121	Proper 24 C	My help comes from the LORD, the maker of heaven and earth. (2)
122	Advent 1 A	I was glad when they said to me, "Let us go to the house of the LORD." (1)
123	Proper 9 B	Our eyes look to you, O God, until you show us your mercy. (3)
124	Holy Innocents	We have escaped like a bird from the snare of the fowler. (7)
124	St. Luke	Our help is in the name of the LORD. (8)
126	Advent 3 B	The LORD has done great things for us. (4)
126	Thanksgiving B	The LORD has done great things for us, and we are glad indeed. (4)
126	Proper 25 B	Those who sowed with tears will reap with songs of joy. (6)
126	Lent 5 C	Those who sowed with tears will reap with songs of joy. (6)
130	Lent 5 A	With the LORD there is mercy and plenteous redemption. (6-7)
130	Proper 5 B	With the LORD there is mercy and plenteous redemption. (6-7)
130	Vigil of Pentecost	There is forgiveness with you. (3)
131	Epiphany 8/Proper 3 A	Like a child upon its mother's breast, my soul is quieted within me. (3)
133	Easter 2 B	How good and pleasant it is to live together in unity. (1)
136:1-4, 23-26	St. Thomas	God's mercy endures forever. (1b)
136:1-9, 23-26	Vigil of Easter	God's mercy endures forever. (1b)
138	Proper 16 A	O LORD, your love endures forever. (9)
138	Proper 12 C	Your love endures forever; do not abandon the works of your hands. (9)
138	Epiphany 5 C	I will bow down toward your holy temple. (2)

Psalm	Day	Refrain
139:1-5, 12-17	Epiphany 2 B	You have searched me out and known me. (1)
141	Nativity of St. John the Baptist	My eyes are turned to you, LORD God. (8)
143	Vigil of Easter	Revive me, O LORD, for your name's sake. (11)
145:1-8	Proper 20 A	The LORD is slow to anger and of great kindness. (8)
145:8-15	Proper 9 A	The LORD is gracious and full of compassion. (8)
145:8-9, 15-22	Proper 13 A	You open wide your hand and satisfy the needs of every living creature. (17)
145:10-19	Proper 12 B	You open wide your hand and satisfy the needs of every living creature. (17)
146:4-9	Advent 3 A	The LORD lifts up those who are bowed down. (7)
146	Proper 27 B	The LORD lifts up those who are bowed down. (7)
146	Proper 18 B	I will praise the LORD as long as I live. (1)
146	Proper 21 C	The LORD gives justice to those who are oppressed. (6)
147:1-12, 21c	Epiphany 5 B	The LORD heals the brokenhearted. (3)
147:13-21	2nd Sunday a. Christmas	Worship the LORD, O Jerusalem; praise your God, O Zion. (13)
148	1st Sunday a. Christmas ABC	The splendor of the LORD is over earth and heaven. (13)
148	Easter 5 C	The splendor of the LORD is over earth and heaven. (13)
149	All Saints C	Sing the praise of the LORD in the congregation of the faithful. (1)
150	Easter 2 C	Let everything that has breath praise the LORD. (6)
Exod. 15:1b-13, 17-18	Vigil of Easter	I will sing to the LORD who has triumphed gloriously. (1)
Deut. 32:1-4, 7, 36a, 43a	Vigil of Easter	Great is our God, the Rock, whose ways are just. (3-4)
Isa. 12:2-6	Vigil of Easter	With joy you will draw water from the wells of salvation. (3)
Isa. 12:2-6	Advent 3 C	In your midst is the Holy One of Israel. (6)
Jonah 2:1-3 [4-6] 7-9	Vigil of Easter	Deliverance belongs to the LORD. (9)
Wisd. Sol. 6:17-20	Proper 27 A	The beginning of wisdom is the most sincere desire for instruction. (17)
Wisd. Sol. 10:15-21	2nd Sunday a. Christmas	We sing, O Lord, to your holy name; we praise with one accord your defending hand. (20)
Song of the Three 35-65	Vigil of Easter	Praise and magnify the Lord forever. (35b)
Luke 1:47-55	Advent 3 A	My spirit rejoices in God my Savior. (47)
Luke 1:47-55	Advent 3 B	The Lord has lifted up the lowly. (52)
Luke 1:47-55	Advent 4 BC	The Lord has lifted up the lowly. (52)
Luke 1:68-79	Advent 2 C	In the tender compassion of our God, the dawn from on high shall break upon us. (78)

Index to *Psalter for Worship, Cycle C*

Psalm	Day	Refrain	Composer	P
1	Epiphany 6/Proper 1	They are like trees planted by streams of water. (3)	Daniel Kallman	
1	Proper 18	Their delight is in the law of the LORD. (2)	Dorothy Christopherson	
7:1-11	St. James the Elder	God is my shield and defense. (11)	Ronald Turner	
8	Name of Jesus	How exalted is your name in all the world! (1)	Michael Hassell	
8	Holy Trinity	Your majesty is praised above the heavens. (2)	Valerie Shields	
11	St. Simon and St. Jude	In the LORD have I taken refuge. (1)	Ronald Turner	
12	St. Bartholomew	The words of the LORD are pure. (6)	Anne Krentz Organ	
15	Proper 11	Who may abide upon your holy hill? Whoever leads a blameless life and does what is right. (1-2)	John Paradowski	
16	Vigil of Easter 3	You will show me the path of life. (11)	May Schwarz	
16	Proper 8	I have set the LORD always before me. (8)	Valerie Shields	
17:1-9	Proper 27	Keep me as the apple of your eye; hide me under the shadow of your wings. (8)	David Cherwien	
17:1-9, 16	St. Stephen	I call upon you, O God, for you will answer me. (6)	Thomas Pavlechko	
18:1-7, 17-20	Confession of St. Peter	My God, my rock, you are worthy of praise. (2)	Thomas Pavlechko	
19	Epiphany 3	The law of the LORD revives the soul. (7)	Daniel Kallman	
19	Vigil of Easter 6	The statutes of the LORD are just and rejoice the heart. (8)	May Schwarz	
19:1-6	St. Andrew	Their sound has gone out into all lands. (4)	Thomas Pavlechko	
22	Good Friday	My God, my God, why have you forsaken me? (1)	Robert Buckley Farlee	
22:18-27	Proper 7	In the midst of the congregation I will praise you. (21)	Valerie Shields	
23	Easter 4	The LORD is my shepherd; I shall not be in want. (1)	Carl Schalk	
25:1-9	Advent 1	To you, O LORD, I lift up my soul. (1)	Carolyn Jennings	
25:1-9	Proper 10	Show me your ways, O LORD, and teach me your paths. (3)	Valerie Shields	
27	Lent 2	In the day of trouble, the LORD shall keep me safe. (7)	Thomas Keesecker	
29	Baptism of Our Lord	The voice of the LORD is upon the waters. (3)	Robert Hobby	
30	Easter 3	You have turned my wailing into dancing. (12)	Carl Schalk	
30	Proper 5	My God, I cried out to you, and you restored me to health. (2)	Valerie Shields	
31:9-16	Sunday of the Passion	Into your hands, O LORD, I commend my spirit. (5)	Robert Buckley Farlee	
32	Lent 4	Be glad, you righteous, and rejoice in the LORD. (12)	Thomas Keesecker	
32	Proper 6	Then you forgave me the guilt of my sin. (6)	Valerie Shields	
32:1-8	Proper 26	All the faithful will make their prayers to you in time of trouble. (7)	David Cherwien	
33:12-22	Vigil of Pentecost	The LORD is our help and our shield. (20)	Robert Buckley Farlee	
33:12-22	Proper 14	Let your lovingkindness be upon us, as we have put our trust in you. (22)	John Paradowski	
36:5-10	Epiphany 2	We feast upon the abundance of your house, O LORD. (8)	Daniel Kallman	

Psalm	Day	Refrain	Composer	Pa
97	Easter 7	Rejoice in the LORD, you righteous. (12)	Carl Schalk	
98	Christmas Day	All the ends of the earth have seen the victory of our God. (4)	Robert Hobby	
98	Vigil of Easter 9	Lift up your voice, rejoice and sing. (5)	Mark Sedio	
98	Proper 28	In righteousness shall the LORD judge the world. (10)	David Cherwien	
98:1-5	Holy Cross Day	The LORD has done marvelous things. (1)	Anne Krentz Organ	1
99	Transfiguration	Proclaim the greatness of the LORD; worship upon God's holy hill. (9)	Martin Seltz	
100	Thanksgiving	Enter the gates of the LORD with thanksgiving. (3)	David Cherwien	1
103:1-5, 20-22	St. Michael and All Angels	Bless the LORD, you angels of the LORD. (20)	Anne Krentz Organ	1
103:1-8	Proper 16	The LORD crowns you with mercy and lovingkindness. (4)	John Paradowski	
104:25-35, 37	Day of Pentecost	Send forth your Spirit and renew the face of the earth. (31)	Carl Schalk	
111	Proper 23	I will give thanks to the LORD with my whole heart. (1)	Dorothy Christopherson	
112	St. Barnabas	Happy are they who fear the LORD. (1)	Ronald Turner	1(
112	Proper 17	The righteous are merciful and full of compassion. (4)	John Paradowski	
113	Visitation	Let the name of the LORD be blessed from this time forth forevermore. (2)	Carolyn Jennings	1(
113	Proper 20	The LORD lifts up the poor from the ashes. (6)	Dorothy Christopherson	
114	Vigil of Easter	Tremble, O earth, at the presence of the LORD. (7)	Robert Buckley Farlee	
116:1, 10-17	Maundy Thursday	I will take the cup of salvation and call on the name of the LORD. (11)	Robert Buckley Farlee	
116:10-17	St. John	Precious in your sight, O LORD, is the death of your servants. (13)	Thomas Pavlechko	9
118:1-2, 14-24	Easter Day	On this day the LORD has acted; we will rejoice and be glad in it. (24)	Carl Schalk	5
119:33-40	St. Matthew	Teach me, O LORD, the way of your statutes. (33)	Anne Krentz Organ	11
121	Proper 24	My help comes from the LORD, the maker of heaven and earth. (2)	Dorothy Christopherson	8
124	St. Luke	Our help is in the name of the LORD. (8)	Anne Krentz Organ	11
124	Holy Innocents	We have escaped like a bird from the snare of the fowler. (7)	Thomas Pavlechko	9
126	Lent 5	Those who sowed with tears will reap with songs of joy. (6)	Thomas Keesecker	3
136:1-4, 23-26	St. Thomas	God's mercy endures forever. (1b)	Thomas Pavlechko	9
136:1-9, 23-26	Vigil of Easter 1	God's mercy endures forever. (1b)	Thomas Pavlechko	3
138	Epiphany 5	I will bow down toward your holy temple. (2)	Daniel Kallman	2
138	Proper 12	Your love endures forever; do not abandon the works of your hands. (9)	John Paradowski	7
141	Nativity of St. John the Baptist	My eyes are turned to you, LORD God. (8)	Ronald Turner	10(
143	Vigil of Easter 8	Revive me, O LORD, for your name's sake. (11)	May Schwarz	4
146	Proper 21	The LORD gives justice to those who are oppressed. (6)	Dorothy Christopherson	8
147:13-21	2nd Sunday a. Christmas	Worship the LORD, O Jerusalem; praise your God, O Zion. (13)	Robert Hobby	15
148	1st Sunday a. Christmas	The splendor of the LORD is over earth and heaven. (13)	Robert Hobby	14
148	Easter 5	The splendor of the LORD is over earth and heaven. (13)	Carl Schalk	57